A Radical Proposal to Reinvigorate the Teaching of the Liberal Arts

A Radical Proposal to Reinvigorate the Teaching of the Liberal Arts

Michael Wayne Santos

ROWMAN & LITTLEFIELD
Lanham • Boulder • New York • London

Published by Rowman & Littlefield
An imprint of The Rowman & Littlefield Publishing Group, Inc.
4501 Forbes Boulevard, Suite 200, Lanham, Maryland 20706
www.rowman.com

6 Tinworth Street, London, SE11 5AL, United Kingdom

British Library Cataloguing in Publication Information Available

Library of Congress Cataloging-in-Publication Data

Names: Santos, Michael Wayne, author.
Title: A radical proposal to reinvigorate the teaching of the liberal arts / Michael Wayne
    Santos.
Description: Lanham : Rowman & Littlefield Publishing Group, [2020] | Includes
    bibliographical references. | Summary: "This book offers a systematic, integrated,
    chronological, multi-disciplinary approach to reinvigorate the teaching of the liberal
    arts and put them back at the center of a student's educational experience"—Provided
    by publisher.
Identifiers: LCCN 2020008458 (print) | LCCN 2020008459 (ebook) | ISBN
    9781475858082 (cloth) | ISBN 9781475858099 (paperback) | ISBN 9781475858105
    (epub)
Subjects: LCSH: Education, Humanistic. | School improvement programs.
Classification: LCC LC1011 .S36 2020 (print) | LCC LC1011 (ebook) | DDC
    370.11/2—dc23
LC record available at https://lccn.loc.gov/2020008458
LC ebook record available at https://lccn.loc.gov/2020008459

For David Lipani, who inspired the idea.

For the students, who deserve the best education
we can provide them.

And, as always, for Mary Colin,
who supports and loves me in all things.

Contents

Preface

The ideas contained in this book grew from my work with my colleague and friend David Lipani. Between the two of us, we have well over seventy-five years of college teaching experience. That is a long time to be doing anything. Over the years we learned a thing or two about teaching and about life. We lived through our share of curriculum revisions and educational trends. Even as David heads toward retirement, the basics have not changed, however.

One of the most fundamental truths is that at the heart of good teaching lie two words: challenge and support. In the classroom, that involves challenging students to think in new ways, to see the relevance of what they are learning for life beyond the classroom, and to support them as they make connections across disciplines.

Which brings me to another truth. Engaging the material and making it "relevant" goes beyond any contemporary emphasis on multidisciplinarity. It necessitates reclaiming the ultimate multidisciplinary experience that has been at the core of Western education for millennia—the liberal arts. This curriculum, flexible and adaptable because of its emphasis on the fundamental issues and questions of humanity, has allowed students to realize their true potential for generations, and despite those who would claim otherwise, has the power to continue to do so.

Living in an age of technology and the rising cost of education, the advent of for-profit universities that promise access to training that will prepare graduates for the careers of the future, and the growing popularity of "massive open online courses," it is easy to forget that. Indeed, these latest trends have left many schools scrambling to be competitive by introducing online classes and adding ever more "relevant" majors. These adaptations reflect the short-term logic of survival, not the long-term thinking necessary to thrive and be excellent, and in so doing, provide succeeding generations the confidence and courage, in the words of Josephus Hopwood, the founder of my institution, to "undertake great works." In essence, to do what should speak to the institutional mission of every college and university.

It is hard work because it requires a fiercely honest examination of teaching practices, student engagement activities, and allocation of institutional resources. Although addressing the surface issues is easier, such an approach is tantamount to ceding control of one's future to others who have radically different agendas, perspectives, and goals. Short-term solutions that ignore the issues central to the mission of a school can only delay the inevitable; they cannot stop its occurrence. As a good friend and colleague once said, "If you are not getting better as an institution, you are dying." Death is unavoidable for us individually. That is not the case for the colleges and universities we serve, unless in our fear of death, we make deals with the devil that abandon the solid principles upon which our institutions were established.

When David and I began discussing what constituted meaningful curricular innovation, we intuitively understood that any program we came up with would have to engage students. That meant challenging them to think, reflect, and address the subject matter coherently, which would allow them in turn to make connections across time and discipline. This would require lots of face time, developing rigorous assignments that demanded reading, writing, and discussion, and putting our students and ourselves into situations that required operating beyond our respective comfort zones. All that just made plain sense.

Be that as it may, we knew one could not build a program on intuition and instinct. So we went about the work of researching high-impact teaching practices, knowing that for a curriculum to be sound, it had to rest on a solid foundation. Lo and behold, we learned some incredible things. Did you know that if you want to get students to read better, you need to require them to read? Or if you want them to write better, you should build writing assignments into your courses? Or did you know that students appreciate timely feedback on assignments and learn better when they can see the connections and relevance of what they are studying for their lives and the other courses they are taking?

No great surprises, right? If you have spent any time in a classroom, on either side of the desk, you know these things. Our predecessors knew these things. So why have there been a multitude of studies designed seemingly to elucidate the obvious? Because what was once obvious has become a lot less so in our sophisticated, high-tech world. Certainly students are different now. Their needs are different. They have experienced different things. Yes, all those things are true, and we need to be aware of them if we want to teach effectively.

But in the pursuit of relevance, we have sacrificed common sense and ignored fundamental truths—that a student is first and foremost a human being. That means that he or she has the same basic needs as anyone who came before. Education, even in an age of Facebook, Twitter, and Instagram, requires work and relationships, with the material, with teachers, and with each other. Reading, writing, discussion, time outside of class with a professor discussing some great idea, all those things are as important now as they were one hundred years ago. They are the stuff that inspires the confidence and courage to undertake great works.

But what of the substance of the education? Here again, it turns out that what is old is new again. The research clearly shows that liberal arts remain at the center of what we need to function in the twenty-first century. That may seem hard to believe, given how we have come to teach them in many of our colleges and universities. Indeed, the undergraduates' predisposition to be uninterested in the general education curriculum because they view the courses as stale, disconnected, and irrelevant reinforces a reality of our own making.

We should know this intuitively because we work in the academy. The research confirms our instincts. So why are we in crisis? Colleges and universities house the best and the brightest. Research, fresh thinking, and innovation are part of the public trust that should be a cornerstone of every institution of higher learning. True enough, but institutions are slow to change, and they are populated by people with fears, vested interests, engrained prejudices, and all the foibles that define humanity as a whole. Beyond that, change is always frightening, and culture change especially so.

Still, the problems remain and we are left with the reality that new thinking —and action—is required. A radical proposal or two needs to be tried, experimentation needs to be done, and open and honest dialogue needs to occur. Our instincts tell us as much, but so too does the data.

We would do well to take some advice from Franklin Delano Roosevelt who, when the country faced a crisis of confidence brought on by the Great Depression, advised, "The country needs and, unless I mistake its temper, the country demands bold, persistent experimentation. It is common sense to take a method and try it: If it fails, admit it frankly and try another. But above all, try something."[1] Certainly the same could be said about not only what the country needs, but about what the educational system that serves it has to do today.

Then as now, the biggest obstacle is the same. As Roosevelt so eloquently put it:

> [T]he only thing we have to fear is fear itself—nameless, unreasoning, unjustified terror which paralyzes needed efforts to convert retreat into advance. In every dark hour of our national life a leadership of frankness and vigor has met

with that understanding and support of the people themselves which is essential to victory. . . .

Compared with the perils which our forefathers conquered because they believed and were not afraid, we have still much to be thankful for. . . .

Happiness lies not in the mere possession of money; it lies in the joy of achievement, in the thrill of creative effort. The joy and moral stimulation of work no longer must be forgotten in the mad chase of evanescent profits. These dark days will be worth all they cost us if they teach us that our true destiny is not to be ministered unto but to minister to ourselves and to our fellow men. . . .

The basic thought that guides these specific means . . . is the insistence, as a first consideration, upon the interdependence of the various elements in and parts of the United States—a recognition of the old and permanently important manifestation of the American spirit of the pioneer. It is the way to recovery. It is the immediate way. It is the strongest assurance that the recovery will endure.[2]

As was the case during the Great Depression, the problem we face as educators is not just economic. Our challenges run deeper than competing for student tuition dollars and worrying about retention. We need, as Roosevelt advised the nation in the early 1930s, to remember our roots and appreciate that a lot of the heavy lifting has already been done for us by our forefathers—those who not only established the country on solid ground, but the institutions for which we work.

The founding principles of American education are solid. Our happiness, our job satisfaction, and our legacy will best be served by recognition of our interdependence and that what we do requires us to achieve and to create. It carries with it a moral obligation that has nothing to do with tenure, promotion, or any of the other material perks afforded by the academy. Finally, whether leaders or led, we must respond to the current crisis with frankness and vigor.

There are no pretensions that this Radical Proposal constitutes a panacea. It is no more the "miracle cure" than was the New Deal. However, if this book helps to stimulate discussion about the issues that face higher education and leads to some bold experimentation, it will have served its purpose. The system is broken and has been for some time. It is well past time that we try something, "and if it fails, admit it frankly and try another. But above all, try something." Certainly we owe nothing less to those who have come before us, to those who will follow us, and to those we now serve.

Acknowledgments

This book grew, as I outline in the introduction, from a collaboration over curriculum reform with my dear friend and colleague, David Lipani of the University of Lynchburg's English Department. He has since moved on to greener pastures—semi-retirement. I, however, remain like a dog with a bone. Every time I see something about the problems confronting higher education or the challenges posed to the liberal arts, or I engage with students in long and meaningful conversations outside class about issues we discussed in class, or even more so when I run into alumni or students on campus that I have not taught in a few years and we fall into discussions and they talk of their ability to make connections because of what they learned in history, I am reminded that what is needed in higher education is what has always been needed—engagement between students and faculty over real issues, which means embracing the liberal arts.

Sick of hearing the mantra, colleagues have encouraged me to set David's and my ideas into a book so that perhaps they can have an impact. So in addition to David, I have to single out my friends Scott Amos, Tracy Simmons, and Phil Stump for being especially persistent, while not nagging, waiting for me to catch up with their wisdom that something needs to be written and shared with a broader audience.

Along those lines, my students deserve a special thanks. They keep me honest and challenge me to keep doing what I am doing and to believe in the core values of liberal education, even when all around us they are under assault. Though they have not overtly encouraged publication of the book since I have not mentioned it to them, my students have implicitly done so by what they regularly tell me about what and how they want to learn.

Carlie Wall, my editor at Rowman and Littlefield, provided invaluable help and guidance through the whole process. Julie Kirsch was there every step of the way and cared not only about the quality of the book, but that as an author, my experience was a good one. I cannot say enough about how painless they made it to bring this book "to life."

Finally, last but by no means least, I have to pay tribute to my wife, Mary Colin. Words are not enough to express my gratitude for having her in my life. As with other books, she suffered through countless requests to "listen to this," was the one who first edited the manuscript, and who unwaveringly supports me in every aspect of my life.

Of course, it goes without saying that any errors are mine alone.

Introduction

"If I Could Do It All Again. . . ."

David, driving back from the paintball field: "So, did I ever tell you what I would do if I had the power to go back and do it all again?"

I hesitate a bit before responding, "Ah, no . . ." maybe expecting a post–midlife crisis revelation. "What would you do differently? Career in Hollywood? I know you love the movies."

"No, I mean about my education."

"Oh! Now this could be interesting. What?"

Before going any further, the reader has got to be asking himself or herself what an English professor (David) and a history professor (me) were doing returning from a paintball field. Easy enough answer. David had long taught a course entitled "Literature and Film of Vietnam" and I have been teaching a class in "America in the 1960s" for at least as long.

So what does that have to do with anything, you may wonder. We hit on the notion several years ago that it was one thing to talk about the experience of the Vietnam War, to have students read about it, to view films about it, to read historical analyses, and even to have veterans come and speak about the realities of the war. We could have in-depth discussions in class and students could write well-researched treatises on the topics we assigned. But there was something missing. As any veteran of any war knows, unless you have been there, you cannot fully understand what it was like, nor can you explain what it was like to someone else.

Short of shipping our students to a combat zone, we devised the notion of spending a Saturday during the semester when we taught our classes running several combat scenarios from the Vietnam War. The students usually go into the experience excited—"Oh boy! Paintball! A fun day in the woods!" Or at least curious: "I've never done that before but. . . ." As we leave in the morning for the field, they are chatting, joking, talking about who is going to get whom. On the ride back, they are tired, dirty, quiet, and in many cases, contemplative. We follow up the exercise in the field with a discussion of what they experienced and a writing assignment that challenges them to connect what they experienced vicariously and safely in the confines of the paintball field with what we have been reading and seeing in films. This experiential dimension of the class has added an invaluable layer of learning to both our courses.

That is what we were doing coming back from the paintball field, but what may seem like an unconventional approach to connect students to subject matter is typical of the way we think. We have constantly looked for ways to engage our students, to get them to realize the importance and relevance of the material we are teaching them. So it should hardly have been surprising that David was thinking not about a missed career in Hollywood, but about how the way he was taught (and by extension I and, we would dare say, most of those reading this book) could be improved upon and made more relevant for our students, and in the process, serve to reinvigorate teaching, and if we dreamed big enough, liberal arts education.

"Chronological learning," David said. "It helps me to put things into context. To see how things developed over time. To see the evolution of ideas. The patterns. I was able to do it on my own over the years, obviously, but it would have been so much better if there had been a structure that encouraged that kind of thinking from the beginning. The general education requirements everywhere are just hit or miss. The students take a bit of philosophy, history, literature, and so on. But where are the connections? They really are not encouraged to make them and a lot of them never do. So no wonder the general education requirements are often resented as hoops to jump through till they get to 'the good stuff' of their majors. And we wonder why liberal arts is on the ropes!"

"As a historian, I've got to agree, but it's not just disciplinary bias," I said, the wheels starting to turn in my head. "You're on to something. So what are you doing next Saturday?"

And so we got together to concoct a plan to rethink how to develop a liberal arts core curriculum. On that next Saturday at David's dining room table, we fleshed out what a chronological interdisciplinary approach to liberal arts might look like. The results yielded a four-year plan that is outlined in table I.1.

A twenty-four credit hour "gen ed" core? Wow! Talk about ways to make folks in the science, technology, engineering, and mathematics (STEM) fields happy. But what of content? What about the liberal arts dimension? How would all the higher purposes that education was supposed to be about be served? Could it be possible that we could have our cake and eat it too? In

Table I.1.   The Initial Plan for the Radical Proposal

Freshman First Semester	Freshman Second Semester
Origins and Cornerstones (3 credits): The origins of humanity, from approximately 3,000 BCE to 350 BCE.	*The First International Age* (3 credits): From approximately 350 BCE to the fourth century CE, exploring the Hellenistic period, ancient India, China, Africa, the Roman Empire, and the rise of Christianity.
Sophomore First Semester	Sophomore Second Semester
Toward a New World Order (3 credits): The transformation of the world from ancient to modern times. In the West, the Middle Ages. In Asia, India and China, new heights of development and sophistication. In Africa and the Americas, cultures developed in near isolation.	*Global Encounters* (3 credits): Fifteenth through the seventeenth centuries, the Renaissance, Reformation, overseas exploration, and the Scientific Revolution.
Junior First Semester	Junior Second Semester
Enlightenment and Revolution (3 credits): Ideas and political change in the eighteenth and early nineteenth centuries.	*Reflections of Modernity* (3 credits): Mid- to late nineteenth century, focused on transformation of the Western political, economic, and cultural landscape amid scientific and technological change.
Senior First Semester	Senior Second Semester
Costs and Consequences of Modernism (3 credits): Late nineteenth to mid-twentieth century, examining changes in science and technology and changing political and international realities—imperialism, WWI, the Russian Revolution, WWII.	*Ideology, Technology, and Global Challenges* (3 credits): 1945 to the present, focused on the continuing search for meaning in the shadow of weapons of mass destruction, instantaneous communication, and economic and environmental challenges.

this age of STEM, was it possible to deliver a *genuine* liberal arts education and meet the economic and practical necessities imposed by the marketplace without selling our souls in the process?

It would obviously take more than a Saturday of brainstorming around a table to answer these questions, but we were inspired to see if we were indeed onto something. So we began to talk to students and colleagues about the idea. They agreed it was worth pursuing. If that was the case, the proposal needed a name. Kicking it around with some of our colleagues, "The Kronos Liberal Arts Core" came into being. The logic was this. In Greek mythology, Kronos (otherwise spelled *Cronus*) was born to Gaia (Earth) and Uranus (Sky), two of the first generation of Titans. After he reached his maturity, he overthrew his father and became leader of the gods. As the centuries passed, and especially when the Romans confiscated the Greek gods and made them their own, Kronos gradually evolved into Chronos, the personification of time; during the Renaissance, he was further evolved into "Father Time."

Hence, *Kronos* refers primarily to time—past, present, and future—but also to power because Kronos/Chronos was chief among the second generation of gods (who gave birth to Zeus, Hades, and Poseidon, among others). The use of the name Kronos, then, was meant to convey the movement of mankind through time as it invented, then embellished, the many disciplines we now value in the educated world, ideas and practices that have aided humanity in reaching the heights of mental prowess, tapping into the power of intellect for the greater good of all.

This was getting at the heart—the CORE—of the liberal arts. By honoring chronology, the program would focus students on the steady march of ideas across the ages. It would honor the power of those ideas as they grew, altered, reappeared, and perpetually shaped their respective epochs. With the knowledge of those seminal ideas, from their birth to their current manifestations, students would be equipped with the fullest means of understanding and contending with their world. It was a lofty goal, but then again, that was *THE GOAL* of liberal education "once upon a time." We had come full circle. Given the challenges confronting society and our students today, that goal is as essential and vital as it ever was.

Which is why the program needed to be framed not as a set of general education "requirements," the "hoops" David so rightly described as he posited the problem in the first place, but as a *CORE*, the *centerpiece* of a student's four-year education. So rather than a bunch of disconnected classes in "liberal arts" disciplines that met a set number of required course hours, or as occurs at some institutions, distribution requirements, Kronos would ask students to take a focused set of courses across their four-year career.

Each class would build on the other, be multidisciplinary by nature, and have logical tie-ins with other more specialized courses that, if students were interested, they could take as electives to explore themes and topics in greater depths within traditional departments. Even if they chose not to do so, that sense of disconnect that left students wondering why they had to take a particular course and how it related to another class in some other field to which they could draw no obvious link other than that both filled some preset, seemingly arbitrary requirements, would be eliminated.

When we talked to students about the idea, they agreed it made sense. Indeed, they were not shy about what they thought about their education, and they instinctively knew what they were missing. Like David, they wished for something different, and were willing to tell us about it. Of course, we were not so naïve as to believe that what they told us was not simply what we wanted to hear. After all, we were their professors. There was the issue of self-selecting bias in our data sample.

So we sought out a randomly chosen cross-section of what our institution's students thought. To ensure objectivity, we asked colleagues with the appropriate expertise to organize and run several focus groups of students and alumni to solicit their opinions about their experiences with the general education curriculum, and to ask their thoughts about a new idea that was being proposed for a liberal arts core. Over and over, the statements about the general education requirements echoed each other along these lines:[1]

- "Some majors . . . require too many hours to finish all general education courses in time to graduate in four years."
- "The general education courses do not allow for students to take classes based on their personal interests."
- "There are inconsistencies among the expectations and requirements of the various general education classes."
- "Classes can lead to confusion about other cultures."

When asked what they saw as the potential benefits of the proposed Kronos Program, the common response was that it afforded the opportunity to "connect ideas and develop problem-solving skills."[2]

Speaking or communicating with alums and students individually, the response was the same. An alumnus spoke for many of his classmates when he wrote, "I've come to various insights over the years from undergrad through grad school, but they've in most cases been haphazard aha moments earned after much trial and error. I would very much have appreciated a general education experience that systematically and purposively helped me see the connections between the issues and disciplines I was studying."[3]

A history major with a minor in education echoed his sentiments, and those of her classmates across campus, when she said:

> I wish that this program had been in place when I came . . . [here]. I'm an education minor and know from my classes that interdisciplinary learning is the most effective approach to education. I also know that as a student, I learn best when I can see the connections between things. Besides, that's how the real world is, so shouldn't we learn that way too? . . . And I love the flexibility of . . . [fewer] hours. If I'd had fewer general education hours, I could not only have met all the requirements for my major and for teacher certification, but there are so many courses I would have taken had I had the chance.[4]

A psychology major noted that she wished that more of her general education classes challenged her to make connections to big ideas and issues:

> The point of a college education, after all, is not getting a bunch of facts that you have to learn or memorize, but to think critically. I have friends who are trying to figure out what they want to do with their lives, what will give their lives meaning besides earning a lot of money. For me, college should be about more than job training. I want to deal with the deeper questions, the things that get at the heart of what it means to be a human being, to live a good life. That's what the liberal arts are supposed to challenge me to do. That's the most important thing I can take away from here. . . . I just wish that that was the case across my entire experience here.[5]

The hit-or-miss nature of the experience that this student addressed is not just a problem at our institution, but at every other school we have heard of, including the ones we knew as undergraduates. Somehow, though, the problem has become more acute since we were students. Perhaps because it has been allowed to fester for as long as it has. Perhaps because of changes in the marketplace. Perhaps because of advances in technology. Coming up with a laundry list of "becauses" ultimately serves no purpose, though, since it does not remedy the problem. So, armed with newfound conviction and evidence that it was not just our perception, we pressed on. That entailed research into the dynamics of the issue not only at our institution, but at the national level, something I will share later in the book.

As the concept unfolded and our information grew, many of our colleagues welcomed the idea and offered their suggestions and input. We encouraged them to do so, and Kronos took on a life of its own. Still, fear is an all-too-human emotion. The fear of the unknown, of what such a "radical" restructuring of the curriculum might do for traditional departmental structures or disciplinary prerogatives, left the proposal nothing more than that. No one was to blame, and what happened to Kronos at our institution I am sure has happened to other proposals at countless other schools across the nation for similar reasons.

Still, the problems persist and we remain riveted by our fear of change. The problems will not go away on their own, and if past is prologue, are likely to get worse. Indeed, if the issue is the survival of small to medium-sized institutions, the answer lies in meaningful program development. The enlightened self-interest of faculty, staff, and administrators calls for nothing less than to try something radical, and if it does not work, as FDR suggested, admit it, learn from it, and try something else.

As individuals supposedly in the business of learning, such an approach should be exciting, because it offers the hope of creating new knowledge, which is, after all, what the academy is supposed to be about. That it could be creating new knowledge that would serve our primary function—to educate future generations—so much the better. And at the risk of sounding overly romantic in this cynical age, is that not our sacred trust?

Since then, David has begun phasing out of teaching, but he and many of our colleagues have urged me to offer Kronos—our particular radical proposal—to a broader audience. In fact, I have been the one who has kept the flame alive, especially every time I hear or read a new story about the dire realities confronting higher education and think that there is at least one solution that we have not yet tried. So I finally have heeded those voices urging me to "speak up" and have written this book.

I see this volume as a conversation starter. If it challenges colleagues at other institutions to ask, "If I could do it all again, what would I do?" wonderful. The more of us who ask that question, the more likely we will come up with a variety of workable "radical proposals," each adaptable to particular institutional settings and each in its own way helping to improve how we teach our students, and by extension, what future they will then be able to create.

Indeed, the question is one that should be asked by anyone concerned about the state of education today, be they in or out of higher education. That means that students and parents at all levels should consider the value of pursuing a Radical Proposal as they search for alternatives to a system that is very broken at all levels. Certainly, they should pose some hard questions as they consider colleges and universities and what they want for their tuition dollars. However, they need to be asking these questions of their secondary schools as well, and demanding that something changes.

Generalists in the media, social commentators, and policy makers who keep a close eye on the state of education should take note of the message, if not all the specific suggestions laid out in this book, for it is well past time that the current discussion about the state of American education move toward concrete programming designed to address the problems. For those within the academy, administrators and faculty who are serious about the crisis facing their institutions, there would be clear benefit from considering the issues and taking up the gauntlet I have thrown down.

After all, the problems are real and systemic, as I suggest in chapters 1 and 2, but the solutions, as they have always been, commonsensical, as I point out in chapter 3. This leads to the nuts and bolts of the matter—a detailed explication of the Radical Proposal as one possible plan to reinvigorate the teaching of the liberal arts, which I lay out in chapters 4 through 7.

And lest the reader think that the plan is a plea to defend outdated and outmoded ways of thinking, celebrating "discredited" Western thinkers, I conclude, as I do with anyone who will listen, with this assertion: the liberal arts, in their purest form, are about human beings. As such, they speak to universal, transcendent, and enduring truths that embrace people across cultures, empowering them to take control of their lives. In doing so, they become advocates for positive change, not victims. That is what liberal education, when done well, has been able to accomplish over the centuries. If we dare reclaim it as our birthright and accept its challenges, it can do so again.

Chapter One

The Current Crisis
in Higher Education

There is little disagreement among students, faculty, administrators, and parents that colleges should produce "specialists" trained in particular disciplines. But what does it mean to be a "specialist" trained at a liberal arts institution as opposed to one who studies at a more technically oriented school? Liberal arts colleges tend to assume that creating a learning environment that exposes students to the humanities, arts, sciences, and social sciences will produce a well-rounded individual, capable of integrating interdisciplinary understanding into his or her life and professional career. How exactly this occurs, however, is not particularly clear. Requiring a set of prescribed general education courses and hoping that students will learn to make the interdisciplinary connections among them is not enough.

Indeed, the very term "general education" tends to denigrate the real importance of why certain areas of study are required of students in the first place. The purpose is more than providing students with a broad sweep of general knowledge that all "educated" people should have, especially should they end up as contestants on game shows like *Jeopardy!* The original intention of what has come to be called "general education" was to provide students a "liberal arts education": that is, an understanding of the subjects and skills that were considered, since fifth-century BCE Athens, essential for a free person to actively participate in civic life.

That this point is missed by many college students should come as no great surprise. Think about the implicit message students receive by the way the curriculum is organized and structured at most colleges and universities. With required general education classes dominating the first two years of a student's experience, a clear message is sent that the "gen eds" are something simply to "get through" before moving on to a major. The problem is compounded by the fact that general education classes are often seen and treated

1

as random and discrete courses, rarely connected to other general education requirements, the stated mission of general education, or to majors.

The liberal arts have long been understood as the best way of providing students with education for life. Indeed, their very essence has allowed us to draw an important distinction between what constitutes education and what constitutes training. As Robert H. Essenhigh, a professor of mechanical engineering at Ohio State University, wrote in *National Forum: The Phi Kappa Phi Journal*:

> [A] major pressure coming into the universities . . . is the increasing insistence . . . that students, when they leave [college], must be able to walk right into some job without any further "training." This sounds so reasonable that what gets lost is that the universities are not in the business of "training." Their business is "educating."
>
> The difference? It's the difference between know how and know why. . . .
>
> The difference, also, is fundamentally that Know How is learning to Think Other People's Thoughts, which indeed is also the first stage in education—in contrast to learning to Think Your Own Thoughts, which is why Know Why is the final state of education. Indeed, both Know How and Know Why are essential at one moment or another, and they interact all the time; but at the same time, the center of gravity of education is and must be in the Know Why. For emphasis in Know How, go to a training college.[1]

Essenhigh's distinctions are nothing new. They date back to Aristotle and have found articulation in the words of Plutarch, Vittorino da Feltre, Thomas Arnold, Albert Jay Nock, and C. S. Lewis.[2] They also inform the modern resurgence of classical education. Susan Wise Bauer has written:

> A classical education . . . has two important aspects. It is language-focused. And it follows a specific three-part pattern: the mind must be first supplied with facts and images, then given the logical tools for organization of facts, and finally equipped to express conclusions.
>
> But that isn't all. To the classical mind, all knowledge is interrelated. Astronomy (for example) isn't studied in isolation; it's learned along with the history of scientific discovery, which leads into the church's relationship to science and from there to the intricacies of medieval church history. The reading of the *Odyssey* leads the student into the consideration of Greek history, the nature of heroism, the development of the epic, and man's understanding of the divine.
>
> This is easier said than done. The world is full of knowledge, and finding the links between fields of study can be a mind-twisting task. A classical education meets this challenge by taking history as its organizing outline—beginning with the ancients and progressing forward to the moderns in history, science, literature, art and music.[3]

There is far more involved here than nostalgia for a halcyon bygone era. First and foremost, national research clearly shows that students are hungry for academic challenge, for an education that will provide them with meaning beyond dollars-and-cents career choices.

Second, any institution dedicated to student learning must be eternally committed to delivering the best possible education possible, not innovating for innovation's sake, but because it is in the best interests of the students it serves. Indeed, if such ideals are not enough to motivate a serious reexamination of how colleges and universities do business, practical considerations should be. Competition is demanding adaptation and reform. With a multiplicity of options, students and parents are weighing their decisions about college carefully. The consequent effects on retention and the allocation of resources are creating real economic pressure for all institutions of higher learning to either deliver on their promise of meaningful educational experiences, or confront a dire future.

The issues facing higher education have been festering for quite some time, though they are only now beginning to receive increased attention from college and university administrators and faculty. With increasing choices, many students and their families are asking whether the cost of a liberal arts education is worth it. Indeed, there are frightening predictions about the future of traditional brick-and-mortar, four-year institutions. According to Nathan Hardin, for example, "In fifty years, if not much sooner, half of the roughly 4,500 colleges and universities now operating in the United States will have ceased to exist."[4]

Aware of this problem, in April 2012 some 250 representatives from higher education and corporations met at Wake Forest University to discuss the value and purpose of a liberal arts education in the twenty-first century. One of the first objectives participants identified was the importance of clarifying what exactly a liberal arts education is. What they agreed on was that "liberal arts institutions can no longer define themselves by the information of which they used to be the exclusive distributors."

According to Davidson College President Carol Quillen, a liberal arts education should be "defined by its aims, not by the disciplines it encompasses." Specifically, that means providing students with the "ability to take a critical and creative perspective to a situation, to structure and defend an argument, to take a global viewpoint:" all of which is to say, to give students the skills "that employers actively seek [in] liberal arts graduates."[5]

Since the system by which these skills have been delivered has not been significantly updated in generations despite the rapidity of change in today's world, institutions are being forced to take a hard look at whether their mission is being served under current operating paradigms. What they are finding, not surprisingly, is a disconnect between what they promise students and what they deliver. As conferees at the Wake Forest gathering concluded:

> University and college leaders are recognizing the need for deliberate and intentional cultivation of the skill sets that are at the core of the liberal arts graduate. . . . It is no longer enough to assume that the traditional curriculum or traditional college experience will provide current students with the abilities and value promised to them with admission—and especially at the tuition prices being charged.[6]

As Wake Forest President Nathan Hatch put it, "our greatest aspiration is also our most sacred responsibility. We must sustain and consistently renew our holistic community of learning. In doing so, we will provide for students the one thing they most desire: to narrow the gap between their professed ideals and the lives they lead."[7]

WHAT STUDENTS ARE NOT LEARNING

In 2011, Richard Arum and Josipa Roksa published a landmark book titled *Academically Adrift: Limited Learning on College Campuses.* What they found was disturbing, although hardly shocking for anyone who has spent any amount of time in higher education: "a pattern of limited learning is prevalent on contemporary college campuses."[8]

Former Harvard President Derek Bok had observed five years earlier that many students graduate "without being able to write well enough to satisfy their employers . . . reason clearly or perform competently in analyzing complex, non-technical problems."[9] The reasons for this abysmal assessment, Arum and Roksa found, were "multifaceted."[10]

So too have been the responses. Two of the more popular have been to pass the buck or to throw up one's hands and say that fundamentally what happens in school does not influence student outcomes. The first of these tends to focus either on the "system," the students, or the preparation that students receive before they arrive at college. This tendency has been fueled in recent years by standardized testing that puts a premium on rote learning and takes teaching out of the hands of instructors by giving control to politicians and bureaucrats with little to no understanding of the educational process.

Retired high school teacher Kenneth Bernstein spoke eloquently to why professors need to be concerned about the K–12 system from which they are getting their students in an open letter in *Academe*. Essentially saying "don't blame me," Bernstein wrote:

No Child Left Behind went into effect for the 2002–03 academic year, which means that America's public schools have been operating under the pressures and constrictions imposed by that law for a decade. Since the testing requirements were imposed beginning in third grade, the students arriving in your institution have been subject to the full extent of the law's requirements. . . .

Now you are seeing the results in the students arriving at your institutions. They may be very bright. But we have not been able to prepare them for the kind of intellectual work that you have every right to expect of them. It is for this that I apologize, even as I know in my heart that there was little more I could have done. Which is one reason I am no longer in the classroom.[11]

There is more than enough truth in what Bernstein said. Indeed, it speaks to the fact that a Radical Proposal needs to be introduced well before students apply to college, and that parents *demand* that it happen. Still, that does not absolve higher education of its part in compounding the problem once those high schoolers hit America's college campuses.

Nor is it correct to buy into the popular notion that, as Arum and Roksa characterize it, schooling is "a mechanism that primarily works to reproduce, exacerbate, and certify preexisting individual-level differences."[12] In other words, if one is born of privilege and attends a highly selective institution, one is naturally going to do better in life than someone from a lower socioeconomic group or who attends a less-prestigious college or university. If that is true, then there is really no point in having any but the most elite attend any but the most highly ranked academic institutions.

Clearly, that makes little sense. Arum and Roksa rightly point out that "students' actions and institutional contexts shape educational outcomes."[13] Put simply, what we expect of our students and how we support their learning make a difference. Unfortunately, the bar has increasingly been set far too low. Students not only enter college less well-prepared than their parents and grandparents did, they expect to study, and actually do study, far less.

Researchers from the University of California Santa Barbara and the University of California Riverside found that full-time students studied forty hours per week in 1961, but only twenty-seven hours weekly in 2004. The drop, they concluded, was "extremely broad-based, and . . . not easily accounted for" by the way questions were posed, by "work or major choices, or [by] compositional changes in students or schools."[14] Interestingly, though, there has been little effect on grade point average or degree completion. As one professor found by "going undercover," students have perfected the art of "controlling college by shaping schedules, taming professors, and limiting workload."[15]

College instructors have been complicit in this, not only because they allow themselves to be "tamed," but because they have struck an informal bargain with their students, which goes something like this, according to

George Kuh: "I won't make you work too hard (read a lot, write a lot) so I won't have to grade as many papers or explain why you are not performing well."[16] In practical terms, the results are self-evident. Students asked to read less than forty pages a week and to do fewer than twenty pages of writing a semester scored far lower on the College Learning Assessment—which is designed to measure critical thinking, analytical reasoning, problem solving, and writing—than did their peers who took classes demanding *both* extensive reading (more than forty pages a week) and writing (more than twenty pages of writing a semester).[17]

THE LIBERAL ARTS AND HUMANITIES AT RISK

All this suggests, as Alexander Astin put it, students "learn what they study."[18] There is more to Astin's statement than mastery of skills, however. It should come as little surprise that with students unable to read, write, speak, or think critically, graduates are leaving school woefully ignorant of the liberal arts, which traditionally have been the cornerstone for promoting these very skills and, more importantly, the values and ideals to function in a democratic society. The reasons for the shift in the focus of the American system of higher education are seemingly reasonable on their face.

There is the economic argument, which asserts that the humanities are no longer relevant in an age of multinational corporations and globalization. Cultural and social considerations hold that the United States has no real literary or artistic canon, so short of affording personal insights and enjoyment, the study of the arts and literature have no real broader function. In an age that glorifies technology and science, the humanities seem irrelevant, vague, and too "touchy-feely." Finally, college academic departments seem to require three things to garner the support of higher education administrators. They must (1) be devoted to the study of money, (2) be capable of attracting serious research money, or (3) demonstrably promise that their graduates will make significant amounts of money.[19] In simple terms, studying the humanities is viewed across the academy as increasingly irrelevant and a waste of both time and tuition dollars.

The results are evidenced in the precipitous decline of students completing bachelor's degrees in the humanities between 1948 and 2011. The shift in student interest to majors in the sciences and business and management has been especially evident since the late 1980s. These trends, as studies by Harvard University and the American Academy of Arts and Sciences have argued, promise to be dangerous to the future of the nation that US colleges and universities seek to serve.[20] The reasons are no mystery.

W. E. B. Dubois reminded his readers over one hundred years ago that "the true college will ever have one goal—not to earn meat, but to know the end and aim of that life which meat nourishes."[21] Put another way, as Andrew Delbanco observed:

> [L]iterature, history, philosophy, and the arts are becoming the stepchildren of our colleges. This is a great loss because they are the legatees of religion in the sense that they provide a vocabulary for formulating ultimate questions of the sort that have always had special urgency for young people. In fact the humanities may have the most to offer to students who do not know that they need them—which is one reason it is scandalous to withhold them.[22]

The realties that have been discovered by researchers on higher education are perhaps more clearly understood outside the academy than within it. Unfortunately, too many in academe are still in denial about an issue that has been fairly common knowledge in the general public for some time: there is a serious problem with the educational system that needs to be addressed. The bottom line is that the public has begun voting with their feet because they see all too clearly that they are being charged exorbitant prices for an inferior product. Market forces cannot be ignored, which make projections like that by Nathan Hardin all too plausible unless something is done immediately.

Chapter Two

The Cost of Doing Business

Unfortunately, students and parents have bought the hype about quick paths to the careers of the future that online, for-profit institutions have marketed to them. And who can blame them? A traditional education at a brick and mortar institution is expensive and requires all those courses that Andrew Delbanco rightly says young people need, but that a competitive, technology-driven, global marketplace seems to have made irrelevant.

The numbers appear to speak for themselves. In 1994–1995, average tuition, fees, and room and board at a four-year public college or university was $10,630 (in 2014 dollars) before grants and aid. By 2014–2015, those costs had reached an average of $18,940, a 56.1 percent increase in twenty years.[1] The figures for private four-year institutions were naturally higher. In 1994–1995, a student attending a private college could expect $26,490 in tuition, fees, and room and board before grants and aid. In 2014–2015, that number was $42,420, a whopping 62.4 percent increase over the same period.[2]

More importantly, such costs carry with them debt implications. In 1995, the average college debt was $13,327[3] (or $20,500 in 2018 dollars, the most recent year for which data could be calculated).[4] By 2013, the situation was even bleaker. Sixty-nine percent of college graduates owed $28,400, (or $30,600 in 2018 dollars)[5] according to the Institute for College Access and Success (TICAS).

Nineteen percent of these individuals had private loans, which were more expensive and had fewer consumer protections. Combine that with the job market and things seemed direr still. The class of 2013 faced a 7.8 percent unemployment rate. If one factored in underemployment, that number jumped to 16.8 percent.[6] But there is a catch-22 built into these statistics. As the TICAS report on student debt pointed out, "recent research underscores the strong employment and earnings prospects for those with college degrees.

On average, four-year college graduates continue to experience far less unemployment and to earn higher salaries than their counterparts with only a high school education."[7]

It is no wonder that students and their parents are looking carefully at how they invest their education dollars. There is a lot at stake, and if part of what they are paying for seems to have little bankable return after graduation, why spend the money and go into debt for it? After all, what does the ability to quote Shakespeare have to do with earning a living or paying off student loans? Although one passage from Shakespeare might be worth remembering: "Neither a borrower nor a lender be."[8] Still, graduating knowing that line from *Hamlet* hardly seems worth it when one is starting out in life facing upward of $30,000 in debt.

Not that pursuing an online education at a for-profit institution stands one in better stead. In 2012, students receiving a bachelor's degree from such schools were 29 percent more likely to have loans than their counterparts who attended more traditional colleges and universities. They also owed, on average, 43 percent more than those who had attended a brick and mortar institution.[9] Still, that matters little when the perception is that one gets more bang per buck by forgoing a liberal arts–based education in favor of career training.

WHAT IS IN A NAME?

Shying away from the dirty business of marketing like the for-profits with their slick TV ads, colleges and universities are falling over themselves in what can only be termed a branding craze. What makes the institution different, unique, special? What catchy logo or buzz words will help attract students to this college rather than to that university? Pay consultants exorbitant fees to come to campus and spend several days, maybe even a week or two, talking with administrators, faculty, and students, and *voila*, a new identity that will set the school apart and save the day will emerge.

Or if one is at a small college, decide to change the name to *university* in the belief that a makeover of stationery and signage will miraculously enhance the school's prestige or attractiveness. The arguments for such a move are myriad. The college has hit some magic threshold number so that it can be called a university. Because it has become a comprehensive institution,[10] having added graduate and professional degrees to stay competitive, and because it is now listed in *US News and World Report* as a university, it should adopt the name assigned to it by others. Moreover, since in many countries "college" carries with it the idea of a trade or vocational school, becoming a "university" will attract more international students.

Apparently, few administrators have paid attention to how many for-profit schools that amount to vocational and technical schools have co-opted the university label—American National *University*, DeVry *University*, ECPI *University*, to name but a few—making the term all but meaningless. Still, like a talisman, they cling to the belief that by changing the institution's name, students from all over will be attracted by this nifty marketing ploy and classrooms and dormitories will magically fill up.

Except it is not that easy. The quick fix seldom is. For example, the need to conform to the *US News and World Report*'s categories fools no one, especially not the folks at *US News and World Report*. According to James M. Owston, a dean at Mountain State University in West Virginia before it closed its doors in 2012, and who was quoted in the *US News and World Report* article, approximately "200 'colleges' have upgraded to 'universities' to reflect the addition of graduate programs but also because it sounds more prestigious." Owston observed that the trend seems to reflect a response to "peer pressure," with schools that are still called colleges "feel[ing] left behind if they're not 'universities.'"[11]

Finding a new name because the "cool schools" are doing it, or developing slick promotional materials without substantive programming that is connected to a clear sense of institutional mission, is at best wishful thinking, or at worst, a reflection of an institution whose administrative and faculty leaders are loath to do the hard work of meaningful introspection and change. As Roger Dooley, a specialist in neuromarketing—which applies brain and behavior research to business situations—has written:

> Sadly, all too many schools have branding messages that are *interchangeable with hundreds of other schools*. Happy students. Engaged profs. An emphasis on innovation. Taglines like "Creating Tomorrow's Leaders." As the market becomes more competitive, these messages won't set a school apart. Each school needs to define what makes its brand different from other schools, and focus relentlessly on communicating that difference.

He went on to argue that the problem has less to do with "incompetent marketers" than with "the school itself," which has "never defined a mission and accompanying strategy that clearly sets . . . [it] apart." Put simply:

> *The entire institution needs to live the brand.* If a college wants to be known for brilliant teaching, then that desire must permeate every aspect of its strategy. Faculty must be recruited and retained based primarily for their instructional, presentation, and mentoring skills. Evaluation must be constant and improvement must be continuous.[12]

The bottom line is that colleges and universities have always had a viable product. However, they have failed to keep it fresh and significant. Now, confronted with the consequences of years of neglect, they are scrambling to change the packaging without doing anything about its content. Slapping "New and Improved" on the same old box of laundry detergent does not make it clean clothes any better. And while some consumers will fall for the hype when it is initially introduced, they will not keep buying the product when they realize that all they are getting is a prettier box or bottle.

That is pretty much the situation confronting many colleges and universities. It has been easier to go through the motions and mouth the platitudes about the virtues of the liberal arts than to do the work necessary to continually deliver them in meaningful ways to new generations of students.

WHAT IS THE BUSINESS OF THE ACADEMY, ANYWAY?

The problem has been exacerbated by the tenure and promotion system, which celebrates and rewards work in narrow research and disciplinary areas that are of little relevance to what students learn or need to know. Indeed, it seems that the mission of many colleges and universities has become to indulge the egos of their professors rather than serve the academic needs of their students.

According to one report dealing with scientific research, 1.8 million scholarly articles are published per year in some 28,000 professional journals. Half are read only by their authors and the journal editors. Ninety percent of those are never cited by other scholars.[13] Even more generous estimates paint a less than impressive picture about the effects of scholarly work. According to economist Dahlia Remler, "Non-citation rates vary enormously by field. 'Only' 12% of medicine articles are not cited, compared to about 82% (!) for the humanities. It's 27% for natural sciences and 32% for social sciences." She went on to state:

> I had a hard time finding the rates at which articles were uncited, because the overwhelming majority of relevant articles were about other things, such as the effect of time windows, different inclusion criteria for citations, whether the Internet has changed citation practices and so on. Those are all good things to investigate, but in the grand scheme of things, they are not as important as the large share of articles going uncited altogether. Another point for academia's critics, who contend that academics worry about small things no one else cares about and miss the big things.[14]

What other business would encourage employees to engage in activities of such marginal effect while ignoring the needs and interests of the customers who help keep the doors open?

In a similar vein, Samuel Goldman, a political scientist at George Washington University, observed:

> Academic specialization is the greatest threat to the study of ideas, literature, and artifacts that we call the humanities. From grad school through tenure review, the institutional structures of departments and universities encourage scholars to pursue short-term projects at the expense of slow reflection, to address a few experts rather than an educated public, and to teach as little as they can get away with. The immediate results are predictable: ever-expanding bibliographies of unreadable and unread publications and course offerings geared toward professors' research projects rather than students' needs. So are the long-term consequences: declining interest and support from undergraduates, parents, administrators, and academics in other fields. . . .
>
> By contrast, no one needs to keep up with the journals to be enlightened by Aristotle, delighted by Cervantes, or challenged by Wagner. In many cases, encounters with the academic literature have the opposite effect. To put it bluntly, academic specialization makes the humanities boring without offering the reward of intellectual progress, let alone clear technological and economic benefits.[15]

Enlightenment not only improves one's quality of life, the ultimate purpose of a liberal arts education, but, as it turns out, it makes one eminently employable. No less a source than *Forbes* magazine, one of America's leading business periodicals, opines:

> We believe that the world's thorniest problems will not be solved—nor will our nation be secure—without an understanding of ethics, cultures other than our own, and what it means to be fully human. And we have seen first-hand that students who complete liberal arts degrees have deeply satisfying—and productive —personal and professional lives.[16]

As such insights are heard from a variety of sources, one cannot help but recall the words of Ecclesiastes: "The thing that hath been, it is that which shall be; and that which is done is that which shall be done: and there is no new thing under the sun."[17] Then again, recalling such an admonition assumes that one has grounding in the great wisdom traditions that are so central to a liberal arts education. And perhaps that explains a great deal. If more people had paid attention to what they were studying in their liberal arts core curriculum a generation or so ago, we might not now find ourselves lamenting the current state of education and arguing for a return to those methods and content that have stood the test of time. But no matter. It is never too late to reclaim the truth.

Chapter Three

What Should Be Common Sense about Education

According to Richard Arum and Josipa Roksa, "Our findings suggest that high expectations for students and increased academic requirements in syllabi, if coupled with rigorous grading standards that encourage students to spend more time studying, might potentially yield significant payoffs in terms of undergraduate learning outcomes."[1] There are common-sense connections here that research simply confirms.

The Center of Inquiry at Wabash College, for example, conducted a National Study of Liberal Arts Education, a longitudinal investigation of a broad spectrum of forty-nine colleges and universities to investigate critical factors that affect the outcomes of liberal arts education. The study focused on the best ways to foster outcomes in the areas of critical thinking, cognition, interest in and attitudes about diversity, leadership, moral reasoning, and well-being by asking "What teaching practices, programs, and institutional structures support liberal arts education?"[2]

To promote positive outcomes in these areas, the Center of Inquiry found that institutions need to encourage good teaching and high-quality interactions between faculty and students. When professors show interest in teaching and student development, provide prompt feedback, have meaningful out-of-class encounters with their students, and are organized and clear in their teaching, there is "predict[able] growth on a wide variety of student outcomes."[3]

Additionally, in the face of academic challenges and high expectations, which include frequency of higher-order exams and assignments, challenging classes and high faculty expectations, and exercises that integrate ideas, information, and experiences, students "tend to grow more on our outcome measures. Similarly, students who report lower levels of these experiences are less likely to grow on the outcomes."[4] Such observations have been mirrored by several reports issued by the Association of American Colleges and Universities (AAC&U), including *High-Impact Practices: What They Are, Who Has Access to Them, and Why They Matter,*[5] *Five High-Impact Practices: Research on Learning Outcomes, Completion, and Quality,*[6] and *Ensuring Quality and Taking High-Impact Practices to Scale.*[7]

Best pedagogical practices are one thing. They work independently of discipline and academic level. What students need to learn and how to structure the ways in which they learn it are something else again. The AAC&U's National Leadership Council for Liberal Education and America's Promise has argued:

> Study in the arts and sciences remain an essential and integral part of a twenty-first century liberal education. But it is time to challenge the idea—tacitly but solidly established in American education—that simply taking a prescribed number of courses in liberal arts and sciences fields is sufficient. Rather, new steps must be taken to ensure the study of these core disciplines prepares students to engage the "big questions," both contemporary and enduring. Study in the arts and sciences should provide students with opportunities to explore the enduring issues, questions, and problems they confront as human beings—questions of meaning, purpose, and moral integrity.[8]

The council argued that to achieve these objectives, "a coordinated effort is needed to ensure that all Americans reach high levels of knowledge and skill" in five areas: science, mathematics, and technology; cultural and humanistic literacy; global knowledge and competence; civic knowledge and engagement; and inquiry- and project-based learning. Cautioning that these foci did not constitute a "menu of course categories," the authors of the AAC&U study argued strongly for the need "to move beyond the fragmented modular curriculum that students already take in the arts and sciences, both in school and college."[9]

The problem lies in something that educators have known in some form or other for a long time. Requiring students to understand the world solely from discrete disciplinary perspectives fails to give them the broad understanding that a liberal arts education promises and that functioning in the real world demands. Known as "silo education" because each area of knowledge stands on its own, students are seldom if ever challenged to see the connections between what they learn in one class and another, let alone how what they are learning applies to their lives or what they plan to do with their futures. Put simply, although silos work perfectly well on farms, they do not belong in classrooms.

William Kilpatrick and John Dewey pointed this out early in the twentieth century.[10] More recently, cognitive scientists using advanced imaging technologies to study brain function have found the "single best way to grow a better brain is through challenging problem solving. This creates new dendritic connections that allow us to make even more connections."[11] Not surprisingly, researchers have found that the best way to foster problem solving is through curriculum that encourages students to see the linkages between various disciplines.[12] The results are greater intellectual curiosity, improved attitude toward learning, enhanced problem-solving skills, and higher achievement in college.[13]

Such conclusions reinforce the related finding that the current system of discipline-based education is not as effective as it needs to be. After all, most real-world problems are multidisciplinary in nature and a silo-based curriculum is simply unable to engage students in real-world situations.[14] This makes discussions and debates over STEM versus STEAM (science, technology, engineering, arts, math) largely irrelevant. As John M. Eger, director of the Creative Economy Initiative and the Van Deerlin Endowed Chair of Communications and Public Policy at San Diego State University, put it:

> The existing silos or disciplines . . . are really irrelevant to finding a job. Math and science and art and music become important to the extent that they are folded into a larger context, and used to solve real-world problems. Only then can the student understand how and why such disciplines are relevant and necessary. Education should not only make young people world-wise and hopefully, ignite a love of learning; it must give our students the skills they need to live a meaningful, productive life, i.e., for most this means a job and a living wage.[15]

ADDRESSING THE ISSUE OF LIBERAL EDUCATION

This has long been the promise of liberal education. The challenges of life in the twenty-first century have only served to give the old truths that gave birth to and sustained the liberal arts for hundreds of years new relevance and immediacy. As the American Academy of Arts and Sciences argued, the current state of education in the United States puts the nation at risk.

Just as other countries have come to embrace the American model of "broad education in the humanities, social sciences, and natural sciences—as a stimulus to innovation and a source of social cohesion," an emphasis on narrow training for the professions is creating a pool of future citizens ill-prepared for the challenges and changes of the twenty-first century, both in and outside the workplace.[16]

The humanities and social sciences are quite simply "the heart of the matter" when it comes to preserving the Republic. They serve as "a source of national memory and civic vigor, cultural understanding and communication, individual fulfillment and the ideals we hold in common."[17]

Consider the implications of the liberal arts for the goals set forth in the Academy's report. Goal 1 calls for Americans to be educated in "the knowledge, skills, and understanding they will need to thrive in a twenty-first-century democracy." For this to occur, emphasis on the humanities and social sciences is imperative because they "provide an intellectual framework and context for understanding and thriving in a changing world. When we study these subjects, we learn not only *what* but *how* and *why*."[18]

Goal 2 advocates fostering "a society that is innovative, competitive, and strong." Echoing the educational research, the Academy asserts that "the ability to adapt and thrive in a changing world is based not only on instruction for specific jobs of today but also on the development of professional flexibility and long-term qualities of mind: inquisitiveness, perceptiveness, the ability to put a received idea to a new purpose, and the capacity to share and build ideas with others."[19]

Finally, Goal 3 argues for the need to "equip the nation for leadership in an interconnected world." An emphasis on the humanities and social sciences is the best way to achieve this objective because these areas "teach us about ourselves and others. They enable us to participate in a global economy that requires understanding of diverse cultures and sensitivity to different perspectives. And they make it possible for people around the world to work together to address issues such as environmental sustainability and global health challenges."[20]

Harvard University, in reviewing its arts and humanities curriculum, came to similar conclusions:

> The need to underscore this nexus of illuminating reception and constructive evaluation by the Arts and the Humanities is all the more urgent given the historical moment we face, a moment characterized by economic, military, ecological, religious and technological challenges of mighty profile. We therefore judge re-articulation of the extraordinary promise of the Humanities to be timely. Our students are preparing to act adroitly in a global environment; they are also preparing to flourish in an austere job market. The Arts and the Humanities are essential on both inter-related fronts, cultural and personal.[21]

Among its conclusions, the Harvard study recommended:

- reaffirm[ing] the critical, yet generalist and interdisciplinary tradition of undergraduate teaching
- enlarge[ing] what we are doing by focusing on the interface between the Humanities and other divisions (notably some of the Social Sciences) or even other schools

• emphasiz[ing] the career paths and job satisfaction that the Humanities do enable, both directly and via professional post-graduate schools.[22]

THE GAP BETWEEN THE IDEAL AND THE REAL

Knowing what constitutes "best practices" and appreciating the power of liberal education has not translated into widespread or systematic reform in America's colleges and universities. The results of the studies cited here, the push to encourage high-impact practices, and calls to reinvigorate the humanities make that fact abundantly clear.

One could continue to provide an elaboration of the bleak findings already documented ad infinitum. Suffice it to conclude an overview of the national crisis with the following data. Students in the class of 2009 represented in Arum and Roksa's study typically met with faculty outside of class only once a month, with 9 percent never meeting with their professors at all. Evidence of grade inflation was manifested in the fact that, although 85 percent of students achieved a grade point average of B- or higher and 55 percent had managed a B+ average or better, the typical student studied less than two hours a day.[23]

Stuart Rojstaczer and Christopher Healy, who researched grade inflation for years, showed this has been a long-term trend. In 1940, 15 percent of students received As, 33 percent Bs, 35 percent Cs, 12 percent Ds, and 5 percent Fs. Thirty years later, the number of As had more than doubled while the number of Cs had dropped by about 15 percent. By 2008, nearly 43 percent of students were receiving As and only about 10 percent were getting Ds or Fs.[24]

Such results do not indicate the existence of the most proficient and intelligent student bodies that have ever graced America's campuses. Rather, it is a sad indictment of the state of higher education where teachers and administrators have abetted students' lack of commitment to academic pursuits while promising them the credentials to succeed in life if only they pay the exorbitant prices demanded by tuitions at even the least selective institutions. Arum and Roksa's observations speak volumes:

> As a college class, they [students] deserve and have earned our sympathy. Unfortunately their inflated ambitions and high aspirations have not institutionally been met by equivalently high academic demands from their professors, nor have many of them found a sense of academic purpose or academic commitment at contemporary colleges. Instead, many students in our study appear to be academically adrift.[25]

HARKENING BACK TO THE FUTURE

Plato observed:

> [C]ertain professors of education must be wrong when then say that they can
> put a knowledge into the soul which was not there before, like sight into the
> blind eyes. . . .
>   [T]he power and capacity of learning exists in the soul already; and that just
> as the eye was unable to turn from darkness to light without the whole body, so
> too the instrument of knowledge can only by the movement of the whole soul
> be turned from the world of becoming into that of being, and learn by degrees to
> endure the sight of being, and of the brightest and the best of being, or in other
> words, of the good.[26]

For 2,500 years, humanity understood the truth of what Plato said and
sought to organize education to that end. To teach was to direct the whole
person, not just his or her mind or body, but his or her very being, his or her
soul, to the pursuit of truth, of good. That did not mean career preparation or
acquiring narrow disciplinary-based knowledge, but seeking understanding
about the meaning and purpose of life. It was holistic education before that
term was ever coined.

Alfred North Whitehead put the matter succinctly: "A merely well-
informed man is the most useless bore on God's earth."[27] Knowledge was
about more than data collection. Its pursuit and acquisition carried with it a
responsibility to be a good person and citizen. In short, its aim was to make
people truly human in the noblest sense of that word.

Colleges and universities were once a vital way-station on the path to
citizenship, career, and to actualizing one's humanity. Institutions of higher
learning were communities of faculty, students, and administrators engaged
in the noble purpose of learning for its own sake and for the sake of the society that the academy ultimately served.

As Cardinal Newman once opined:

> [I]ndependent of direct instruction on the part of Superiors, there is a sort of self-
> education in . . . academic institutions . . . ; a characteristic tone of thought, a
> recognized standard of judgment . . . which, as developed in the individual who
> is submitted to it, becomes a twofold source of strength to him, both from the
> distinct stamp it impresses on his mind, and from the bond of union which it cre-
> ates between him and others—effects which are shared by the authorities of the
> place, for they themselves have been educated in it, and at all times are exposed
> to the influence of its ethical atmosphere. Here then is a real teaching . . . [that]
> tends towards cultivation of the intellect; [that recognizes] . . . that knowledge is
> something more than a sort of passive reception of scraps and details.[28]

The need to reclaim the best in our educational heritage speaks to something fundamental for both the individual and society. Socrates once said that the only thing that distinguished him from his fellow Athenians was that he "knew that his wisdom is in truth worth nothing."[29] Understanding his ignorance, he also appreciated that he could neither presume to know what he did not, nor simply accept his ignorance as an excuse not to ask questions, for as he is oft quoted as saying, "the life which is unexamined is not worth living."[30]

Unlike many of his contemporaries, Socrates realized that truth was not easily found or contained in platitudes. The Sophists of Ancient Athens taught rhetoric, which was about convincing people of the truth of their position regardless of how much or how little truth was contained in their arguments. In that, they seemed like modern politicians. With the populace accepting as truth what the Sophists and the politicians said, they followed their leaders blindly, making the state (which reflected the will of the people—after all, Athens was a democracy) like a mindless steed. According to Socrates, such a situation necessitated a gadfly to make things uncomfortable enough to move people beyond their tendency toward slow, steady, unquestioning plodding.[31]

Then as now, left to their own devices, every person seeks their own version of the truth, not *THE TRUTH* as envisioned by Socrates. As a result, individual truths have always been a function of limited perspective—personal, disciplinary, political, religious, and so on—which in turn determines how problems are identified and solutions sought. In a free society, as James Madison observed, individuals seek out those of like mind, which inevitably leads to factionalism and further blinds them to any truth but their own.[32]

The human tendency to seek easy answers to complex social, political, and economic issues, and the natural impulse toward faction, has been exacerbated in the age of cable, Facebook, Twitter, and Instagram. Modern media allows, and indeed encourages, individuals to become insular in the ways that that they see the world, seeking out and finding only those of like mind, while vilifying those with whom they disagree.

The cure for this new form of Sophism requires that colleges and universities graduate critical thinkers capable of conceptualizing life in broader terms, and thus functioning in, and contributing to, a complex, ever-changing world. That means developing a long-term multidisciplinary approach to learning, because only such an approach has the power to encourage the eschewing of simple answers by demanding that the hard questions be asked, just as Socrates did.

The ancients understood that fact. So did the Founders of the American Republic. After all, it was Thomas Jefferson who wrote:

> History, by apprising them [citizens] of the past, will enable them to judge the future; it will avail them of the experience of other times and other nations; it

will qualify them as judges of the actions and designs of men; it will enable them to know ambition under every guise it may assume; and knowing it, to defeat its views.[33]

Seen from that perspective, the distinctive contribution of the United States to the history of liberal education has been to deploy it on behalf of the cardinal American principle that all persons have the right to pursue happiness, and that "getting to know," in Matthew Arnold's words, "the best which has been thought and said in the world" is helpful to that pursuit. That understanding of what it means to be educated is sometimes caricatured as elitist, but in fact it is quite the opposite, as Arnold makes clear by the phrase with which he completes his point: "and through this knowledge, turning a stream of fresh and free thought upon our stock notions and habits."[34] Knowledge, in other words, helps citizens develop the capacity to think critically about the present—an indispensable attribute of a healthy democracy.

The Radical Proposal simply builds on very real strengths, both as they currently exist and as they have been historically manifested. It speaks to the roots of civilization and of the nation, and to the trust that educators have in serving as keepers and disseminators of culture and knowledge. It seeks to build on all that the academy does well and has done well for generations. It is premised on an age-old commitment to challenge students to grow, to learn, to aspire, to stretch, and to become more than they ever thought possible. The Proposal's logic is grounded, quite simply, in a tried-and-true tradition that has served humankind well for over 2,500 years.

If the hope is to grow future generations that are healthy, well-balanced, responsible, and ethical, there is no better way than to plant any proposal dealing with curricular reform in the fertile soil that has anchored the cultural and institutional roots of society for so long. Or, perhaps, to continue the botanical metaphor, there is a clear need to graft such reform to a tree that already has strong and deep roots, the tree of liberal arts.

Chapter Four

A Radical Proposal

The Radical Proposal is a concrete step in the direction of envisioning change. If even *some* of what is proposed here were tried, the culture of higher education and of campus life would be transfigured. Just the act of generating discussion and experimentation would serve that purpose. How could it not, for it would be driven by a clear sense of *mission* regarding the purpose of liberal education and its meaning for students. A transformation would be inevitable.

Imagine one could create a college or university from scratch. How would it be done? That is in essence what the program asks, for it gets to the heart of what every school needs to consider, whether new or long established. Any educational institution should be organized primarily around the curriculum and the type of student it wishes to graduate. In fact, that should be uppermost in any faculty member's and administrator's mind, even when the wolf is not at the door.

The logic here is simple. Such attention to the fundamentals would automatically put in motion a whole new set of dynamics. Indeed, a whole new college experience for faculty, staff, administrators, and students would become theoretically possible. And being possible in its entirety in theory, if even a portion of it could be brought into reality, how much better for everyone.

THE CURRICULUM

It is self-evident, as well as borne out by the research, that to truly appreciate the human experience in all its complexity, the various disciplines need to be brought *together* to simultaneously and systematically examine the human story revealed through the sweep of history. Resorting to discrete disciplinary segments does damage to the interconnectedness of knowledge, to the humanity that created it, and ultimately to the goals of liberal arts education and the skills students need well beyond their four years at college.

The Annales School of history was the first to recognize the importance of the broad sweep of history when writers like Marc Bloch and Lucien Febvre began incorporating social scientific methods into the study of history after the First World War. Fernand Braudel built on their work in the second part of the twentieth century with the concept of the *longue durée*. According to Braudel, historians needed to focus on long-term historical structures, not just the events of the past. In doing so, they come to grasp the all-but-permanent or slowly evolving structures against which individual events transpired, creating meaningful syntheses of understanding.[1]

This approach stands in sharp contrast to the archives-driven research of what some have called micro-historians, who fixate on the study of specific chronological periods and events, often losing the forest for the trees in the process. By examining human knowledge as separate and unconnected, as current general education programs do, we commit the same fallacy that Braudel identified among historians. The core outlined in this chapter adapts the concept of the *longue durée* to create a four-year integrated program of courses that will help students to create the meaningful syntheses we want them to take away from a liberal arts education.

This strategy makes both intuitive sense and is backed by pedagogical research, as has been discussed earlier. In the proposed program, students would examine the various *sides* of an idea, using a variety of disciplinary perspectives to do so. The key would be that they would do so throughout their four-year college education, thus allowing them to develop an understanding not only of the multifaceted nature of human knowledge, but of its evolution and connectedness over time. In this way, they would acquire the cultural, social, and historical contexts that have informed important ideas over the centuries.

REDEFINITION OF THE CAMPUS CLIMATE

The success of such a program would depend on promoting an environment of collegiality across disciplines, focused on developing partnerships among faculty and students. And in the interest of full disclosure, that would mean it would likely work best at small to medium-sized colleges and universities, where tradition and size would facilitate the kind of thinking and cooperation it would require.

By stretching outside their disciplinary comfort zones, faculty would discover new things, think in new ways, and model lifelong learning for their students. Students, in turn, would be able to discover the complexity of the human experience by bringing to bear a multiplicity of disciplinary perspectives to the themes that they explored in the liberal arts core.

Both professors and students would make connections across disciplines, across time, and with each other, as they examined the complex interconnectivity of our global heritage. In the process, each would achieve something of value—greater insight, skills that were transferrable well beyond the classroom, and the satisfaction that once defined life for all members of the academy, be they student sojourners or resident scholars.

To keep the program fresh and alive, to ensure that faculty had a sense of "ownership" over what was taught, it would be essential that those involved in the program participate in regular workshops to discuss readings, assignments, and other issues of pedagogy, sharing what worked and what did not, and thus keeping the curriculum crisp. Additionally, the system would need to remain open to new faculty who wished to join the program, with mentoring by veterans put in place to facilitate the process of entry and participation.

Faculty teaching in the program would also have the latitude to shape the way in which course content was delivered to take account of individual teaching styles, disciplinary strengths, and student learning styles. The goal in all this would be to encourage collegiality across disciplines by reinforcing what all faculty share: a common commitment to excellence as teachers. While whatever evolved in the form of collegial relations could be fostered in part by formalized programming, much of it would, and to be sustainable would need to, grow naturally and organically. However, once established, a positive feedback loop would be created, allowing faculty to take the results of their learnings about content and pedagogy back to their classrooms, both inside and outside the program.

At a systemic level, data collected from faculty gatherings would naturally be used to inform adjustments made to the program as it evolved and developed. Finally, in the case where faculty felt that a course could be improved by other disciplinary perspectives or where nonprogram instructors might be willing to participate in the program on an ad hoc basis to enhance content, there would be opportunities for cross-pollination of ideas about both subject matter and pedagogy beyond the program's learning community.

The core courses would thus be generated, revised, and sustained by those who taught them, all working closely together to achieve the program's goals. In focusing on what they have in common across disciplines—delivering a quality education to students—collegiality would transcend the artificial barriers that have too often kept faculty fragmented despite the relatively small size of their schools.

Fostering a sustained conversation among faculty about the issues central to their professional lives—their pedagogy and their disciplinary interests—would inevitably be a logical outcome of the program. In the case of the first, professors would have the opportunity to develop techniques that not only enhanced what they did in their courses inside and outside of the program, but often do so collaboratively. In the case of the second, faculty would be able to share the passion and insights they have for their specialties with an audience—their colleagues—who were eager to learn, not only so that they could more effectively deliver the content of the core to their students, but because of the excitement of learning for its own sake.

The last reason is perhaps the most compelling, since for many who entered education, the love of learning is what drew them to academic life in the first place. What better model can teachers provide their students about the importance of what they do, and what they want young people to learn, than to demonstrate their own eagerness to expand their understanding of the world?

For both faculty and students, then, a spirit of inquiry would drive a cooperative spirit of learning. No one can be expected to know everything, and certainly the core cannot encompass every facet of human knowledge and experience. However, by taking its cue from the liberal arts, the program would foster a collaborative exploration of the important themes, traditions, readings, thoughts, and writings of the global heritage. In doing so, those involved with the program would become learners as well as teachers, taking responsibility for their own and the community's growing understanding of the subject matter—the focus of the core curriculum.

DOLLARS AND CENTS AND OTHER PRACTICALITIES

Any institution has built-in fixed costs, from physical plant to salaries to tenured faculty positions. At the schools where a program like this would work, liberal arts professors are one of these. As luck would have it in this age of STEM, their classes are required to fulfill general education or distribution requirements, but unfortunately their upper-division offerings all too often go under-enrolled. By branding a liberal arts core as central to the college or university's mission, these salaried individuals—who represent a fixed cost, especially if they are tenured— could be "repurposed" in a way that served students, and thus the institution's mission, in a demonstrable and meaningful way. Just as significantly, it would give the professors a renewed sense of professional direction, with a concomitant effect on morale.

Moreover, as faculty from the humanities and social sciences taught in the program, they would likely generate interest in their upper-division specialty classes, with the positive fallout that that would have both for themselves and for students. For the institution, which tends to calculate the cost efficiency of courses based on bodies in seats, all this would be a plus, since it would now see a more efficient use of its faculty without any capital outlay. Individual departments would, meanwhile, find new audiences among students who would see their offerings as relevant to their education.

Finally, it does not take much research to find that there are a plethora of granting agencies interested in funding innovative programming in education, humanities, and the liberal arts. Given that simple fact, a program like this could bring in money for years to come for both individual faculty and program development, all the while ratcheting up the institution's profile, visibility, marketability, and thus "brand."

THE CORE CURRICULUM IN DETAIL

There are a multiplicity of great ideas around which such a proposed liberal arts core could be organized. Mortimer Adler identified 103 great ideas that he believed "constitute the vocabulary of everyone's thought."[2] Boiled down to their essence and to concepts that can be traced coherently across time, six themes emerge: Nature, Human Nature, Faith, Reason, Values, and Social Organization.

Could the list be changed, expanded, redefined? Without a doubt. But one has to start somewhere. And given the flexibility that needs to be built into a living program like the one under consideration, no doubt these would evolve with time, as did Adler's list, which started with six great ideas, albeit different from the ones suggested here.[3] So following are the themes and their definitions, for the purposes of the program as currently envisioned:

- *Nature:* The word *nature* is derived from the Latin word *natura*, or the "essential qualities, and innate disposition" of things. *Natura* is a Latin translation of the Greek word *physis*, which originally related to the intrinsic characteristics of plants, animals, and other aspects of the physical world. The concept later also came to mean the physical universe. As such, it is a good theme with which to begin. It is nature, in all its meanings, that human beings have sought to understand and control and from which life itself originates. The powerlessness of humankind in the face of natural forces has given birth to conceptions of divinity and of faith. The beauty of nature has inspired great art and literature. Curiosity about the workings of the universe has fostered the development of science. The seeming order that exists in nature has raised questions about the natural laws that govern the physical universe. It has also inspired speculation about the existence of natural laws that govern human relations, giving birth to philosophical and religious musings about ethics, morality, and justice. All these themes resonate across time because they are eternal, derived from the very nature of human beings.

- *Human Nature:* As soon as humans were able to think, they began to puzzle not only about the world around them (nature) but about themselves. This has led to an age-old quest to understand what characterizes human nature. At our core, are we good or bad? Are we rational or irrational beings? Are we mere animals or something more? What is to be made of humanity's ability to think, feel, and act? Boiled down to their essence, these questions provoke wonder about what characteristics are distinctly human, what causes them, and how fixed they are across time and culture. The implications for ethics, politics, philosophy, and theology are enormous and have found countless expressions in art and literature. The quest to understand self also has given rise to historical study, psychology, sociology, and a host of other disciplines traditionally associated with the humanities and social sciences, not to mention studies in the natural sciences.

- *Faith:* According to Hebrews 11:1, "Faith is the substance of things hoped for, the evidence of things not seen."[4] This seems as good a definition as any for the human impulse to seek answers and understanding about a world and universe that can only be understood, as Plato observed, unclearly at best. Foreshadowing the ideas of St. Paul, Plato noted: "For there is no light of justice or temperance or any of the higher ideas which are precious to souls in the early copies of them: they are seen through a glass dimly; and there are few who, going to the images, behold them in the realities, and these only with difficulty."[5] With this a given of the human condition, people have turned to conceptions of God or gods, of divinity, of the transcendent, to explain what they could not fully grasp through reason or their senses. The search for meaning that has resulted has given the world its great religious traditions, has inspired art and literature, and has given inspiration to ethics and morality. It has also sometimes set itself up against the other human tendency to seek answers through reason.

- *Reason:* There is much in nature and the universe that is knowable through rational analysis, and it is this characteristic of human nature that we define as reason. Using logic and observation, humans have expanded their grasp of themselves and their environment. The use of reason has informed the creation, development, and advancement of philosophy, science, language, mathematics, and art. It has fostered the development of law and human notions of progress. It has inspired technology and the organization of political, social, and economic institutions. Finally, it has both complemented and challenged the lessons taught by faith about truth, goodness, evil, justice, ethics, and morality.

- *Values:* The questions that have led human beings to seek answers about who they are and how they fit into the universe have inevitably led to answers that become the basis for personal and societal values. Notions of right and wrong, of justice, of beauty and ugliness, of good and bad, are all products of humanity's quest for understanding. They also evolve naturally from the interplay between the human desire for answers and self-expression and the particular context of time, space, and culture within which that quest for meaning occurs. The influence of values informs notions of truth, justice, wisdom, duty, honor, happiness, and sin, which in turn shapes how any given person or civilization views and creates art and literature. It also defines the way politics, economics, and law are organized and implemented in any particular place and time.
- *Social Organization:* Ultimately, human beings are social animals. They live, interact, and seek meaning within specific social contexts. That means that as they organize government, they seek to understand its purpose, meaning, and function in terms of their attitudes about human nature, about right and wrong, about good and evil, and about justice and injustice. These notions have been derived from values born of faith and reason. They have also come from the opportunities, challenges, demands and realities imposed by the natural order and by humanity's understanding of that order. Thus ideas of democracy, oligarchy, liberty, and equality, to name just a few, are functions of social and environmental realities and their interaction with human concepts that evolve from an ongoing search for meaning. Likewise economic concepts of supply and demand, price, market, monopoly, capital, and trade, or social notions of family, class, custom, and convention are products of this dialectic relationship between environment and human understanding.

These themes would be explored in eight courses, organized chronologically, and taught over the student's four-year career. The structure, elaborated from table I.1, appear in tables 4.1 and 4.2.

There is a need to require what, for lack of a better word, might be called *skill courses*, in addition to this "core," to complete a "general education" that would result in a "well-rounded individual" ready to meet the challenges of today's globalized world. After all, it could fairly be argued that students need to be fluent in at least one foreign language, should have mathematical competency, the ability to communicate effectively both orally and in writing,

Table 4.1.   The Core Curriculum: Freshman and Sophomore Years

Freshman First Semester	Freshman Second Semester
Origins and Cornerstones (3 credits): Examines the origins of humanity, tracing its evolution from approximately 3,000 BCE to 350 BCE. Students will explore how humans came to understand nature and themselves, developed faith and values, learned to think rationally, and organized themselves into ever more complex social systems.	*The First International Age* (3 credits): Focusing on the period from approximately 350 BCE to the fourth century CE, this course examines the Hellenistic period, ancient India, China, Africa, the Roman Empire, and the rise of Christianity as a means of understanding how humans interacted across cultures and adapted their understandings of nature and themselves, their faith, and values.
Sophomore First Semester	Sophomore Second Semester
Toward a New World Order (3 credits): Introduces students to the major themes in the transformation of the world from ancient to modern times. In the West, a synthesis that had begun to take shape in the Ancient World was redefined and modified by the introduction of new peoples and religious forces to lay the groundwork for modern society. In Asia, India and China reached new heights of development and sophistication. In parts of Africa and the Americas, cultures developed in near isolation from the rest of the world.	*Global Encounters* (3 credits): Between the fifteenth and seventeenth centuries, the European synthesis born of the Middle Ages set in motion economic, political, and social changes that established the foundation for the Renaissance, Reformation, overseas exploration, and the Scientific Revolution. Students will examine the dramatic consequences of new or rediscovered ways of thinking on life in Europe, Asia, Africa, and the Americas.

have at least a working appreciation of how a lab science works, and some would argue, a sense of their physical health and well-being.

But those are concerns that need to be dealt with by individual faculties on the ground at their particular institutions, for they are the ones who best know their students. Indeed, with some of these skills, they are issues that could be dealt with at the student level. Given that, further discussion of any specific requirements beyond the core fall outside the scope of this book.

CREATING OPPORTUNITIES

Given the number of disciplines requiring approximately sixty credit hours or more, and the desire of many students to develop two or more areas of study by pursuing an additional major or minors, this program would offer them the flexibility to do so easily while being true to the spirit and purposes of the

Table 4.2.   The Core Curriculum: Junior and Senior Years

Junior First Semester	Junior Second Semester
Enlightenment and Revolution (3 credits): Students will consider the ideas of selected Enlightenment thinkers whose work in political theory, moral philosophy, and economics transformed Western, and eventually global, ways of thinking. They will also examine the eighteenth- and early nineteenth-century revolutions that ushered in the beginnings of modern politics, economics, and society.	*Reflections of Modernity* (3 credits): This course focuses on the transformation of the Western political, economic, and cultural landscape. As science, technology, and industrialization redefined life, people sought meaning and understanding in a variety of ways, both traditional and modern. Against this backdrop, the realities of power and economics will be examined to understand how they shaped class, race, and gender relations.

Senior First Semester	Senior Second Semester
Costs and Consequences of Modernism (3 credits): While technology and science continued to redefine everything from ways of thinking and understanding to how people interacted, old perspectives and national rivalries and aspirations informed the backdrop against which change unfolded. As industrialization made production of new weaponry possible, it turned the twentieth century into the most deadly in human history. Students will consider the resulting irony that, as humans gained more control and understanding of the universe, they found the ultimate meaning and purpose of life more elusive.	*Ideology, Technology, and Global Challenges* (3 credits): The continuing search for meaning has occurred in the shadow of weapons of mass destruction, instantaneous communication, and economic and environmental challenges. In many ways, the modern era has been a combination of constancy and change. As technology continues to push out the envelope of what is possible, the fundamental concerns of humanity continue to demand answers. This will be the central focus of discussion in this course.

liberal arts. With parents and students concerned about the value of a liberal education relative to career preparation, the number of elective opportunities offered by this approach would also provide students the chance to engage in internships and other professional activities, thus increasing their competitiveness in the job market. Moreover, because they would have more room for choice under the demands of this program, students wanting to hone their skills in writing, speaking, mathematics, and performance, areas that are vital in today's competitive economy, could do so by taking classes in those areas.

Additionally, since twenty-first century market realities demand global awareness, the program's flexibility also lends itself to long- or short-term study-abroad experiences. Finally, if one of the goals of the liberal arts is to produce a well-rounded and balanced individual, just creating "breathing room," as the proposal does, would allow even heavily prescribed majors to indulge in some electives where students could pursue something about which they were passionate or just simply curious.

As Guy Claxton, who has written extensively on the connection between the human mind and learning, reminds us, educators need to be about the business of "creating a culture in classrooms—and in the school more widely—that systematically cultivates habits and attitudes that enable young people to face difficulty and uncertainty calmly, confidently and creatively." One of the keys to achieving that end is to help students "discover the things that they would really love to be great at, and strengthening their will and skill to pursue them." This will turn them into lifelong learners and help unleash the type of creativity they will need to succeed in the future.[6]

Parents intuitively understand that and want their children to have the full breadth and benefit of a college education. As one website dedicated to the concerns of parents of college students advised, tell your student to:

> *Take some classes that you love.* Almost all colleges have "all college" or general education requirements. There will also be requirements for your student's major. There may be requirements for a minor if your student has one. Students can feel overwhelmed and focus only on what *needs* to be done. This is important and good. However, encourage your student to also do something that she loves and to do it early in her college career. Too many students think they need to wait until junior or senior year to take a "fun" class and by then are burned out. Encourage her to make room in her schedule for that dance class, art class, sports class, or whatever else might feed her passion for something. This will help her keep balance and give her an important outlet.[7]

The flexibility afforded by a program like the one being suggested would allow students to do just that, and in the process enhance the learning styles that will serve them well for life. If students are more engaged in what they are learning, are curious, and have a passion for what they are studying, that can only serve to benefit everyone. Clearly students will get more out of their college experience, which will positively affect retention and, as marketing and word-of-mouth spreads, recruitment.

Relatedly, faculty will have students in their classes who want to be there and who want to be challenged. Departments will attract students to their courses who might become majors, minors, or at the very least, who will take several classes in their discipline, improving the importance, visibility, and institutional support available to various academic programs across campus. Such an outcome can enhance morale, foster a shared institutional mission across the various stakeholders at any institution committed to delivering a quality education, and build a truly inclusive learning community.

BUILDING COLLEGIALITY

The Radical Proposal would offer a place to begin thinking anew about old ways of knowing. Still, what is suggested in this chapter is clearly not intended as a *fait accompli*. That is a positive thing, because it puts responsibility for program development and implementation squarely on the shoulders of those at any school that wishes to adopt it. After all, that is where it belongs, for they are the ones best suited to know their own needs. And here is where the real collegiality envisioned by the ideas outlined above can begin to take shape, if faculty are willing to see each other as partners in a common endeavor and administrators and staff help to foster and encourage the work.

For it to succeed anywhere, a program like this needs faculty ownership, and that means faculty involvement in its creation and evolution, most fundamentally in the area of curriculum development. The structure, organization, and specific readings suggested for each core course, then, would change as the program faculty hashed out the nitty-gritty of what they would teach.

Specific changes emerging from faculty suggestions would occur within the broad outlines of the program's six central themes and each course's general focus, but as indicated earlier, since the program would be in a constant state of evolution, these too would likely change with time and practice. It would also make sense to pilot the concept to work out the kinks and try out ideas before committing the institution to a wholesale revision of the curriculum all at once.

With general faculty approval, those instructors planning to teach in the program would be granted release time or stipends to accomplish two things: (1) develop concrete means of reaching the program's goals and objectives and (2) finalize the syllabi for core courses. Grants and fellowships for these sorts of activities could be incentivized and the end results easily used to help brand the college or university moving forward in this brand-conscious environment. More importantly, the branding would be tied to the institution's mission of providing quality education, which could only result in something substantive that would have long-term *meaningful* educational and institutional sustainability.

Beyond that, work to develop and maintain a common, living, relevant, liberal arts core as the heart of the institution would foster an intentional and ongoing dialogue among faculty—those teaching and those who would be teaching—so that each instructor in the program had a clear understanding of how his or her class fit in the overall scheme of the core. This would ensure consistency between sections and continuity and connections across the four-year curriculum.

Additionally, periodic meetings of all program faculty—including those who had not yet taught—would encourage colleagues to learn from each other not only about content, but about what worked and what did not in the classroom. Toward these ends, program instructors would be encouraged to visit one another's classes as often as their schedules permitted.

Just as exciting, as the program became part of the institution's educational focus, creating a common experience for all students, even nonprogram faculty would be drawn into the common discussion of ideas as genuine multidisciplinarity permeated the campus culture and fostered meaningful discussions across disciplines. At the very least, all faculty could expect a certain baseline of knowledge from their students and could, with some degree of confidence, expect them to bring that with them to their preparation for any discipline-specific course.

Chapter Five

Addressing Objections to the Proposal

There is a certain knee-jerk reaction to a classical approach to education. It is too elitist and thus irrelevant; it is culturally, racially, or gender biased; it can only be taught by specialists with the skill sets to properly instruct students on the nuances of Shakespeare, Aristotle, or the host of other "masters" who are essential to a well-rounded education. All of these are fallacious and self-serving arguments designed to justify the particular peccadilloes of those advancing them.

The first usually is the go-to argument of institutions marketing a quick education that will prepare students for a career in as short a time as possible. Although vocational education has its place, there is more to higher education as preparation for life than simple job training. If one-third of one's life is spent at work and one-third sleeping, then what one does with the other one-third is significant. Being blind to that fact and assuming that making money and mastering technology is all there is constitutes a clear and present danger.

The second argument assumes that the so-called "Western canon" is biased and exclusive. Although there is truth in that assertion, it ignores the beauty of the liberal arts. Much in the Western canon is transcendent because it speaks not to culturally specific themes and issues, but to universal human ones. Questions of faith, reason, social justice, and morality are not culturally or temporally bound. Moreover, the canon has the ability to be, and should be, expanded because it is driven by its focus on humanism. It is its openness that has kept the discussion fresh, which has challenged people to think and ask questions. Indeed, it was the basis for civilization itself across the planet in all its myriad forms. Without it, there would be nothing upon which to build, and nothing upon which to hope.

The third argument promotes the very elitism that reinforces the backlash of the first two arguments, but has reflected within it the insecurity of academics seeking to justify their own existence. One must be honest. The humanities are about human beings, not specialists opining about the meaning of a particular passage of literature or philosophy for other academics in an obscure professional journal that few will read but that will count as a publication come tenure or promotion time. Historians, philosophers, and scholars of all stripes love to wax eloquently on all manner of issues that they have become experts upon, but in the end, that have little relevance either for the real meaning of their discipline, or for those who sit before them wanting, or being required, to learn.

If faculty took a minute to reflect, and asked themselves why they entered the profession in the first place, most would say to learn new things—to be stretched and to be challenged. How can students be expected to do the same if their teachers are not willing to model it for them?

This can seem daunting at first blush. "The System" encourages discipline expertise. Graduate programs are all about specialization. But even so, there is no such thing as a "pure" anything professor in the humanities. Everyone who teaches a liberal arts–related class steps outside his or her discipline on a daily basis, or at least they should. Faculty in, say, literature courses refer to historical facts and figures routinely; they make use of art work and philosophy and music to help emphasize their point. Professors of philosophy or religion have to account for political movements, famous men and women, contemporary issues, and cultural phenomena of all sorts. How much do any of these individuals know about the disciplines to which they might refer? Enough to make them useful and meaningful, and that is what students need to learn.

TAKING THE LEAP

To teach in a program like the one proposed here, humanities faculty would engage themes and ideas within and beyond their own disciplines across time, just as they likely already do as a matter of course in their regular classes— and as they expect, or ought to expect, their students to do. Contrary to popular belief, that does not require graduate-level understanding of a period or author or theme but rather general knowledge of the sort well-educated individuals already have, would like to have, should have, or can acquire.

To approach teaching in this way simply requires remembering what it means to be a humanist. That means heeding the advice of historian Steven F. Hayward and not getting caught up in self-importance. A teacher's job is to guide students along the way. As Hayward put it:

Since most of the humanities do not require the close classroom instruction in technical skill like organic chemistry, how about having students in English, history, philosophy, and other humanities courses meet for the first month of classes *by themselves*—no professors, no teaching assistants. Just appoint a discussion leader from the class and then read and discuss the texts (original texts only—no textbooks) amongst themselves.[1]

Even though the Radical Proposal does not go as far as that, Hayward does well pointing out that the humanities, at their best, can be done by *anyone* because they speak to everyone. That is because the liberal arts are about consilience, or the unity of all knowledge. Perhaps the notion of consilience was no more clearly expressed than by Edward O. Wilson, who argued, "The greatest enterprise of the mind has been and will always be the attempted linkage of the sciences and the humanities. The ongoing fragmentation of knowledge and resulting chaos in philosophy are not reflections of the real world but artifacts of scholarship."[2]

Wilson offered an interesting perspective on the true state of human understanding, especially in light of the focus of the Radical Proposal:

Disciplinary boundaries within the natural sciences are disappearing, to be replaced by shifting hybrid domains in which consilience is implicit. These domains reach across many levels of complexity. . . . Each in an industry of fresh ideas and new technology.

Given that human action comprises acts of human causation, why should the social sciences and humanities be impervious to consilience with the natural sciences? And how can they fail to benefit from that alliance? It is not enough to say that human action is historical, and that history is an unfolding of unique events. Nothing fundamental separates the course of human history from the course of physical history, whether in the stars or in organic diversity. Astronomy, geology, and evolutionary biology are examples of primarily historical disciplines linked by consilience to the rest of the natural sciences. History is today a fundamental branch of learning in its own right, down to the finest detail. But if ten thousand humanoid histories could be traced on ten thousand Earthlike planets, and from comparative study of those histories empirical tests and principles evolved, historiography—the explanation of historical trends—would already be a natural science.[3]

The organizing principle of the Radical Proposal readily acknowledges that human knowledge can only be understood in this broader context, reaffirming what the ancients knew long ago, or as Thales so eloquently put it:

Of all things that are, the most ancient is God, for he is uncreated.
The most beautiful is the universe, for it is God's workmanship.
The greatest is space, for it holds all things.

The swiftest is mind, for it speeds everywhere.
The strongest, necessity, for it masters all.
The wisest, time, for it brings everything to light.[4]

WHY THIS PROGRAM?

The core ideas governing the program being proposed recapture what was truly good and academically salient in the past and make them relevant for the current climate. Certainly, students are interested in professional training. However, the research and the long-standing traditions of liberal education clearly speak to the need to dismantle the false dichotomy between professional and general education. The latter complements and enhances the former and, indeed, speaks more to the fullness of life for which college should prepare students than any narrowly construed professional training. It is, quite simply, what education is supposed to do.

There are other, less academic considerations that need to be confronted because they not only affect institutional morale, but they ultimately impinge on what happens in the classroom. What used to characterize academic communities has either vanished or been greatly diminished. Faculty have become more insular, less collegial, more protective of their narrow pursuits, and less concerned and devoted to the general welfare of their students.

There is no doubting that there is an abundance of fine teachers, but it is probably fair to say that many among them put forth their most concerted efforts into upper-level courses within their disciplines, while regarding general education classes in much the same way that undergraduates do—something to be endured until they can focus on the "good stuff." This does not mean that *all* faculty are guilty of dismissing their general education classes, but it does suggest that those classes often receive far less attention than they deserve. And perhaps for good reason. It is human nature for people to be passionate about the things that interest them and to give less attention to those things that are demanded of them.

However, in such calculations, what is forgotten is the thing that binds a faculty at any institution regardless of specialty. They are all teachers, professional educators. Although the approach required by the Radical Proposal would not necessarily work at what the Carnegie Classification of Institutions of Higher Education used to call an R1 University, or as it is currently categorized, an RU/VH (a research university with very high research activity),[5] that is not where the work of the traditional liberal arts core has traditionally been done, nor where a radical proposal like this would likely succeed.

It is in the small to medium-sized school where a passion for helping students learn was first encouraged, and where a renaissance in the liberal arts, if it is to occur, needs to begin. The first step is to rekindle an environment that reminds faculty, staff, and administrators of that truth, that rewards a commitment to undergraduate education in all its dimensions in concrete ways, and that celebrates the fact that students, faculty, administration, and staff are a community of learners.

WHAT IF IT DOES NOT WORK?

One thing professors and administrators at small and medium-sized institutions share with those laboring in the research university is the pursuit of knowledge. Experimentation around the model being proposed would generate knowledge. The national trends are frankly rather bleak. Still, there is hope. Students want to be challenged. They realize that they are missing something and are hungry for more than what the educational system has thus far provided them.

Research suggests that the answer lies in a revitalization of the liberal arts, once again making the big questions that have historically challenged students to think, to read, to write, and to make connections central to a college education. That does not mean requiring a general education that offers a cafeteria approach to a variety of different disciplines in the misguided assumption that students will see connections and cultivate a deeper understanding of their world and themselves, all the while honing the skills they will need to function in life. Rather, it involves development of a systematic liberal arts core organized around what research has demonstrated are high-impact teaching practices.

Clearly, something must be tried to better meet the needs of students and of the various institutional missions of schools across the country. Given current research and the wisdom acquired through 2,500 years of human education, the Radical Proposal represents a logical approach to addressing the problems facing American education. Still, it would be foolish to pursue it on a whim, which is why, in the tradition of the academy as generator of knowledge, this is being offered as a challenge to educators to offer amendments, implement all or parts of the program, and critique and discuss the results.

No matter the outcome, a program organized around the ideas put forth by the Radical Proposal will create new knowledge about the best and most effective ways of teaching future generations. Perhaps some institution will implement the program in its entirety and completely validate its logic and thus afford an alternative option for many students, both nationally and internationally.

Perhaps institutions and individuals will take some of the ideas and dabble with them, adapting them to their particular learning environments, yielding successes and failures, and in the process report on both. These findings can be used to modify education at all levels, to improve even on the best practices, and to foster effective ways of delivering the liberal arts to meet the ever-changing realities of the twenty-first century.

Of course, there is always the chance that a program of this kind will prove unworkable. People could find the ideas contained herein completely ridiculous, but in doing so, develop better alternatives. In such a scenario, that too would be a benefit, since it would yield real, meaningful knowledge that would have practical benefit for how students are served. Whatever the case, no one will ever know until something along the lines proposed is tried, and certainly whatever learning comes from the experiment will stand education and the nation in good stead moving forward.

Chapter Six

The First Two Years of the Program

A Student's-Eye View

Imagine a college that decided to implement the Radical Proposal. But first, a few caveats. What follows is intended to provide the reader with what *could* be possible. There is no attempt to describe every detail of curriculum, every reading, and every assignment. Suffice it to say that "high-impact" practices would drive the organization of the curriculum and the structure and organization of assignments. To provide a sense of what that would be like, the textbox entitled "Inside the Classroom" give an up-close-and personal look at how some of the issues narrated in the text for each semester would be handled. Every term would be organized around classes like the ones showcased. Just as significantly, many of them have been field-tested by the author, so based on a sample of one instructor, they should work!

Finally, there is the need to address the obvious objection that there is no way to "cram" everything in. One would be surprised at what a little creativity can do. For example, the so-called "flipped classroom," which emphasizes students getting a lot of the "content" outside the classroom while valuable in-class time is used to engage the material and make connections, can work wonders. Of course, that still involves a lot of out-of-class face time with students, setting up mentoring sessions with peers, and making sure there are resources aplenty for them to draw on, but that is what has always gone into good teaching. And it pays off with student learning, which is why they are called *high-impact practices*.

Even so, decisions will have to be made as to what to include and what to leave out. That is where the themes come in. Coverage is less important than the spirit of the liberal arts embodied in the materials and the topics discussed. Which brings up a related matter: the readings. Faculty would likely be arguing about what to include, and given the breadth of choice in the "canon," would have some discretion as to content from class to class and from year to year. However, the discussions that informed program content would keep it fresh for those who taught it, and in turn, for those being taught. In that way, the liberal arts would be what they were meant to be—living, breathing, and engaging.

Finally, notice that the themes are highlighted in *italics* on the pages that follow. This is to remind the reader what would be emphasized to students on a regular basis—the *connections* between the course content and the themes of the core.

FRESHMAN YEAR

A freshman has signed up for *Origins and Cornerstones*, the first class in the Liberal Arts Core. The class description says the class "examines the origins of humanity, tracing its evolution from approximately 3,000 BCE to 350 BCE. The course explores how humans came to understand nature and themselves, develop faith and values, learn to think rationally, and organize themselves into ever more complex social systems." It is part of a program that is supposed to study the interplay and links between themes and the relevance of various disciplines for seeing the world, helping students to build connections across time, see the dynamic tension among the ideas that have shaped and continue to shape the world, and cultivate an appreciation for the value of various disciplinary perspectives for an understanding of the human condition.

For the average first-year student, that would all sound like so much mumbo-jumbo, and he or she would likely wonder what exactly that has to do with anything *real*. But since the tuition is paid, and in the overall scheme of things, there are only twenty-four hours of these core requirements to get through, what the heck?

First Semester

Students are exposed to the origins of civilization around the world and are asked to consider the connections between these ancient civilizations and the development of the foundations of human ways of knowing (*faith* and *reason*) and *social organization*. They are challenged to consider the role of *faith* in shaping how early peoples came to understand the forces of *nature* that affected their ability to farm; how they came to understand themselves (*human nature*) in relationship to a higher power; how they interacted with each other and organized themselves politically (*social organization*); how their beliefs created concepts of right and wrong, good and evil (*values*); and how these notions were translated into literature and a sense of history. Finally, they are asked to examine how the necessities of survival created by *nature* and the demands of civilization (*social organization*) inspired technological innovation through the use of *reason*.

In addition to employing the obvious—the tools of Religious Studies (a guest speaker from that department would have attended class, and students would be encouraged, and in some cases required, to attend lectures by Religious Studies faculty)—the methodologies and questions asked by historians, political scientists, economists, and scholars of international relations have been used to explore issues of government organization and cross-cultural contact and conflict.

In fact, students might attend a symposium sponsored by the program on the Amarna period in which members of the International Relations, Economics, and Art Departments discussed the international world order that existed when the Egyptians, Assyrians, Babylonians, Hurrians, Hittites, and Mycenaean Greeks dominated the eastern Mediterranean World (*social organization, values*). The experience might awaken an awareness of the fact that people who lived that long ago were not all that different—for they too were part of a global economic and political network.

With any luck, the images of artifacts from the period that the students see will make them think about art in a whole new way. Or maybe they will be motivated to look into that Study Abroad trip to Greece that they have heard advertised and that some of the upperclassmen have been talking about.

In class, students will examine sacred scripture from the Old Testament through the lens of literary analysis and criticism because their instructor happens to be an English professor. That is after she invites her colleagues from the History and the Religious Studies Departments to discuss the historical and religious significance of the Old Testament (*faith, values, human nature, social organization*). For those with professors in history or religious studies, someone from English will be invited to class to lead a discussion on the Bible as literature.

From there, the focus shifts to the role of *faith* during the golden age of Greece, juxtapositioning Greek conceptions of divinity with that of the Middle East and other parts of the world. In examining the causes of the difference, students consider the challenges and opportunities provided by *nature* on the Greek peninsula, Mesopotamia, the Levant, Asia, and Africa.

Nature's impact on *social organization* (for example, the role of mountains in Greece for the development of the city-states vs. the need for large-scale organization demanded by the agrarian-based societies of Mesopotamia) and conceptions of humanity's ability to understand (*faith, reason*) and control (*nature*) the environment is examined with an eye to explaining why the Greeks tended to cultivate rationality (*reason*). Students learn that in Greece, and especially in Athens, this impulse was reinforced by the structure and dynamics of life in the polis (*social organization*).

**TEXTBOX 6.1. INSIDE THE CLASSROOM:
FIRST SEMESTER, FRESHMAN YEAR**

Lesson on Virtue

Note: Students have been given background on Ancient Greece and the causes and course of the Peloponnesian War during the preceding class.

Class 1:

Out of Class Assignment: Read "Pericles's Funeral Oration," from Thucydides, *The History of the Peloponnesian War, Book I*; "The Melian Dialogue, from Thucydides, *The History of the Peloponnesian War, Book V*; Socrates's *Apology*.

Synopsis: Pericles praised Athens for its virtue, saying, among other things, that "where the rewards of virtue are greatest, there the noblest citizens are enlisted in the service of the state." However, when the Melians appealed to the Athenians on the grounds of virtue and honor to respect their pleas for neutrality during the Peloponnesian War, they were told, "the powerful exact what they can, and the weak grant what they must." As if to bear that out, Socrates was put to death for asking questions, believing "that the greatest good of man is daily to converse about virtue."

Out of Class Assignment: (1) Write a paragraph reaction to each reading. (2) Post three questions to the class raised by the readings.

In-Class Activities: Students discuss the events attendant to the Funeral Oration, the Melian Dialogue, and Socrates's trial using the questions they have submitted. The professor directs the conversation to the question, "Does virtue matter?"

Class 2:

Out of Class Assignment: Based on the class discussion and the readings, write a paper answering the question: "Does virtue matter?"

In-Class Activities: Students discuss their essays. The class is broken up into four groups. Groups 1 and 2 are assigned the task of recreating Socrates's trial. Groups 3 and 4 are assigned the Melian Dialogue. The "prosecution" in Socrates's trial will seek to refute his assertion "that the greatest good of man is daily to converse about virtue," while Socrates defenders will seek to make the case for virtue. The Athenian group in the Melian Dialogue scenario will be seeking to prove that "the question of justice only enters where the pressure of necessity is equal," while the Melian group will argue the opposite. All groups are free to draw on any material from the course that they have discussed, not just the readings for this assignment.

Class 3:

Out of Class Assignment: Groups work on preparing their positions with help of the instructor and from upper-class peer mentors.

In-Class Activities: Socrates's trial is conducted. Groups 3 and 4 serve as the "jury" and are sworn to impartiality. The instructor serves as the judge. When the jury has reached a verdict, the class discusses the results of the trial.

Class 4:

In-Class Activities: The Melian Dialogue is conducted. Groups 1 and 2 serve as the "jury" and are sworn to impartiality. The instructor serves as the judge. When the jury has reached a verdict the class discusses the results of the exercise. The larger implications of the four classes are then explored with an eye toward understanding the Greek way of knowing, as well as the enduring human questions they raise for us as individuals and society.

By this point, students begin to appreciate connections to the liberal arts as they understand that the birth of the humanist idea that placed emphasis on life in the here and now occurred in Athens and marked a major development in the evolution of Western *values*. They become involved in some interesting discussions and debates as a result, particularly when attention shifts to the Greek conception of *human nature*, since it was the Greek understanding of humanity that grew logically from their natural and social environments (*nature, social organization*) and shaped much of their contributions to philosophy, literature, and political thought (*reason, values*).

As the semester draws to a close, students might attend a production of *Antigone* by the Theatre Department, then discuss its lessons in class (*values, human nature, social organization*). A faculty member from the Communications Studies Department would give a guest lecture on rhetoric to supplement the reading of Aristotle's treatise (*values, reason*) on the subject, and a member of the Biology Department would do likewise on Aristotle's work in biology (*reason, nature*). One of the students' final class assignments would be to explore Greek ways of knowing.

It would be difficult for even the most cynical freshman to go home at the end of the semester and not be surprised at how much he or she learned. Some may even have had their interest piqued enough to start thinking about taking a class from one or more of those professors they heard from during the fall. He or she might even look forward, strangely enough, to next semester.

Second Semester

Students are back on campus and this time the freshmen are enrolled in *The First International Age.* It focuses "on the first international age from approximately 350 BCE to the fourth century CE . . . explor[ing] the Hellenistic period, ancient India, China, Africa, the Roman Empire, and the rise of Christianity as a means of understanding how humans interacted across cultures and adapted their understandings of nature and themselves, their faith, and values."

They pick up where they left off in December: the tension between *faith* and *reason*, only this time beginning in the Hellenistic world, then moving to the Roman Empire, and then on to an examination of the rise of Christianity. After that, the focus shifts to the non-Western world, juxtapositioning developments in the West with concurrent events in India, China, and Africa. Students are challenged to think about some interesting new issues as they consider the influence of the rise of empire and cosmopolitanism (*social organization*) on *faith* and philosophy (*reason*) as well as the reciprocal effect of the latter two on political organization (*social organization*).

They are presented with some fascinating examples for contrast and comparison: the unifying effects of Buddhism on the Mauryan Empire in India, of Christianity on the Roman Empire, and of Confucianism on China. The realities of the Kush and Egyptian Empires, which they discussed during the first semester, are explored more fully in the period of their decline.

Against this backdrop, the instructor asks students to think about how philosophers and religious thinkers conceptualized *nature* and *human nature*. In one assignment, they compare and contrast the Cynical, Epicurean, and Stoic (*reason*) views on *nature* and humanity (*human nature*) with the spiritual aspects of these notions articulated by Hinduism, Christianity, and Buddhism (*faith*). It should become clear to them that the *values* of individuals in these cultures were affected in fundamental ways by these *faiths* and philosophies (*reason*). The professor makes a point of emphasizing the complex interplay of these factors, making clear the difficulty of easy categorization or platitudes.

To reinforce that point, just when students think that maybe things are making some sort of sense, the instructor throws in another set of issues to consider: "What," she asks, "do you make of the values of Confucianism (*reason*) and Taoism (*faith*)? What are the implications of these perspectives for a 'Chinese world view,' if one can define such a thing?" All this leads to an interesting series of discussions about both the commonality of the human experience that gave birth to *faith* and *reason*, and the role that environment (*nature*) and culture (*social organization*) have had in shaping the answers that each society developed. By the end, students realize they are engaged in the age-old debate over nature versus nurture.

TEXTBOX 6.2. INSIDE THE CLASSROOM: SECOND SEMESTER, FRESHMAN YEAR

Lesson on Chinese Ways of Knowing

Note: Students have been given background on the Axial Age, when the world's wisdom traditions seemed to be developed in a few centuries almost simultaneously in China, India, and the West. They have also been exposed to the cultural, social, and political contexts surrounding these developments.

Class 1:

Out of Class Assignment: Read Selections from Confucius, *The Analects.*

Synopsis: The assigned selections emphasize that people's values should be based on morality, tradition, and a natural love for others. Confucius's social philosophy rested on development of an ideal he called *ren* that embodied a ubiquitous state of virtue, which, although no living human being has yet attained it, should be something toward which everyone strives. In *The Analects* he speaks with his students, providing examples of *ren*, and makes the point that one should be careful not to engage in artful speech and ingratiating manners that would create a false impression of one's character. He also advised, "Do not do to others what you would not like done to yourself."

Out of Class Assignment: (1) Write a paragraph reaction to the reading. (2) Post three questions to the class raised by the readings.

In-Class Activities: Students talk about *The Analects* using the questions they have submitted. The discussion focuses on two points: (1) The parallels between Confucius's preoccupation with *ren* and Socrates's preoccupation with virtue, which is, in essence, the same issue; and (2) What has been called Confucius's reverse Golden Rule—"Do not do to others what you would not like done to yourself"—and Jesus's Golden Rule—"Do unto others as you would have them do unto you." What does this say about the transcendence of certain human issues versus the power of culture to shape and inform how humans understand themselves, others, and the world? This discussion is cast within the context of the Axial Age perspective.

Class 2:

Out of Class Assignment: Read Selections from Lao Tzu, *Tao Te Ching.*

Synopsis: The assigned selections, like Taoism itself, defy easy characterization, and herein lies the essence of the Tao. Or, to quote briefly: "The way you can go is not the real way / The name you can say is not the real name. . . . [T]he wise soul does without doing, / teaches without talking. / The things of this world exist, they are; / you cannot refuse them. / To bear and not to own; / to act and not to lay claim; / to do the work and let it go; / for just letting go / is what makes it stay. . . . To know what endures is to be openhearted, magnanimous, regal, blessed, following the Tao, the way that endures forever. . . ." Thus, "True rulers are hardly known to their followers. . . . The good the truly good do has no end in view. . . . People despise orphans, widowers, and outcasts. / Yet that is what kings and rulers call themselves. / Whatever you lose you have won. / Whatever you win, you have lost."

Out of Class Assignment: (1) Write a paragraph reaction to the reading. (2) Post three questions to the class raised by the readings.

In-Class Activities: Students talk about the *Tao Te Ching* using the questions they have submitted. The discussion focuses on the two points from last class, only with more specificity. There is a commonality running through Confucius's idea of *ren*, Socrates's focus on virtue, and Lao Tzu's idea of living in harmony with the Tao. At their heart they all speak to a counterintuitive idea of selflessness, the Golden Rule in some form. The professor reminds students to recall the teachings of the Buddha, which they have also examined in a previous class, and again the Axial Age perspective is raised.

Class 3:

Out of Class Assignment: Beginning as early as the Han Dynasty, and fairly well institutionalized by the Tang Dynasty, Civil Service Examinations, premised on knowledge of Confucian logic, became the standard for government advancement and cultural continuity in China until 1905. This was an arduous process for which people studied long and hard. Students now have the chance to put themselves in the place of ancient Chinese students. Since the examinations occurred over several days, two days are allowed for "Mock Exams."

EXAM DAY 1. Answer these questions: (1) The Zhou and Tang dynasties had weak central governments and strong local governors while Qin and Wei dynasties were the opposite. Discuss the advantages and disadvantages of these two. (2) ZhuGe Liang did not have the heart of Shen Buhai and Shang Yang (both Legalists—who advocated manipulation of power and politics and brutal enforcement of the law), but used their methods. Wang Anshi used their methods but did not want to admit it. How do you assess these men?

In-Class Activities: Students discuss their answers to the Civil Service Examination, applying the teaching of *The Analects* and *Tao Te Ching*.

Class 4

Out of Class Assignment: EXAM DAY 2. Answer these questions: (1) Schools are made for three reasons: to educate the people, train talented people, and revitalize the industries. Which of these three is the most important? (2) The Great Learning teaches to illustrate illustrious virtue, to renovate the people, and to rest in the highest excellence. However, now we see local prefects often cheat and lie to the central government. How may we put an end to this kind of practice?

In-Class Activities: Students discuss their answers to the Civil Service Examination, applying the teaching of *The Analects* and *Tao Te Ching*. Contrasts between Eastern and Western answers to the broader questions of virtue and the role of government are also considered, since students have also explored the ideas of the Stoics, Cynics, and Epicureans and have examined the histories of empire under Alexander, the Romans, Qin Chi Huang Di in China, and Ashoka in India.

Over the course of the semester, as during the first term, professors from History, Philosophy, and Religious Studies contribute in one way or another to discussions inside and outside of class, but the cross-cultural focus of this semester exposes students to faculty from three more departments: Sociology, Economics, and Mathematics. The first gives a lecture on the interplay of ideas and social structures and how they facilitate cross-cultural interaction (*social organization, reason*).

One of the Economics professors comes to class and speaks about the economic effects of empire, noting the parallels, albeit on a far smaller scale, to the modern globalized economy (*social organization*). As if to drive that point home, the professor from the Math Department points out, in a program symposium that explores the major contributions to mathematical understanding that have occurred as a result of the work of thinkers in Alexandria and the Mauryan Empire, that this period constituted a sort of premodern explosion of STEM learning (*reason, values, social organization*).

As the first year draws to a close, students realize that they have learned a whole lot more than they thought they would have from this Liberal Arts Core. Many have gotten a big leg up toward their major, and even had room in their schedules to explore some other classes they would never have considered had they not taken these two core classes. In fact, at the urging of their advisors, some have signed up for the "Greek Civilization" course being offered by the History Department in the fall and "Religions of Asia" in the spring, which is being taught by the Religious Studies professor they met at one of the program's events. This first year likely will have left many students wondering what is in store next.

SOPHOMORE YEAR

First Semester

Students are signed up for a course titled *Toward a New World Order*, which the catalog describes as introducing them

> to the major themes in the transformation of the world from ancient to modern times. In the West, a synthesis that had begun to take shape in the Ancient World was redefined and modified by the introduction of new peoples and religious forces to lay the groundwork for modern society. In Asia, India and China reached new heights of development and sophistication. In parts of Africa and the Americas, cultures developed in near isolation from the rest of the world.

The themes of *faith* and *reason* students explored in their freshmen year are again a central focus of discussions on medieval Europe because a millennium of religiosity defined most of life in that time and place. Everything from art (*values*) to politics (*social organization*) were affected by the particular doctrinal teachings of the Catholic Church, they learn. Even so, rationality did not disappear. It was just rechanneled to other purposes, as scholasticism and the works of St. Thomas Aquinas attest. Whether derived from *reason* or *faith*, medieval notions of right and wrong, good and evil (*values*), shaped how Europeans thought about *human nature*, about themselves, and about people of other regions. As students reflect on all this, their professor leads them to a startling revelation—that the liberal arts were being shaped and formalized in new ways in new institutions called universities.

Students examine two interesting and very different pieces of literature, Dante's *Divine Comedy* and Chaucer's *Canterbury Tales*. The Divine Comedy provides a perspective on the medieval world view as influenced by the Catholic Church. An allegory about the soul's journey toward God, the work draws heavily on the insights of Thomas Aquinas, which makes sense, given what they just learned about scholasticism. But then *The Canterbury Tales* is a whole different thing. Students are asked to think about the difference between the two works from a literary, philosophical, and religious perspective, paying particular attention to the contrasts between them and what they teach not only about medieval ideas and society but about modern conceptions of spirituality (*faith*) and *human nature* (*reason, values*).

The focus of the course then shifts to the Middle East, where parallel developments were occurring. The rise of Islam that sprang from the Abrahamic religions of Judaism and Christianity (*faith*) offered an alternative view of the world (*values*) and threatened the fragile political and social infrastructure of Europe, while creating one of its own (*social organization*). This simultaneously preserved the achievements of Ancient Greece and Rome and contributed to the advancement of mathematics (*reason*). Students are asked to attend a panel discussion outside of class on the state of modern Middle Eastern politics, then in class seek to place contemporary issues into their broader historical context.

Before closing out this part of the course, they consider the irony that the conflicts over *faith* between Christianity and Islam helped bring about the demise of Catholicism's stranglehold on Europe. In the quest to recapture the Holy Land during the Crusades, the Church encouraged major transformations in the political and economic structure (*social organization*) of Europe, reopened contact with the Far East, and with it, caused the death of one-third of the European population by the bubonic plague, the result of unforeseen exposure to microbes to which they had no immunities (*nature*).

The guest lecture on infectious diseases, by a professor from the Biology Department, sets the context for students to examine connections they may never have thought of before. In the following classes, they are asked to wrestle with the effects of epidemics at a personal and social level by studying art focused on death motifs. What happens when medicine does not have the answers? How would they and society deal with the real possibility of death, painful, sudden, unpredictable? (*values, human nature, nature, social organization*) These are the questions raised in class, made all the more real by the Covid-19 pandemic. Assignments challenge the students to relate to people who lived long ago, and realize that they are not that different when things are boiled down to their basics—like the stark realities of life and death.

Still, the professor says, something positive came from all this darkness. He reminds the class that humanity is no longer mired in that dark place. The devastation helped to transform *values* and lay the groundwork for the modern world. Students figure that must be true, but they will have to wait until next semester to see how specifically.

TEXTBOX 6.3. INSIDE THE CLASSROOM: FIRST SEMESTER, SOPHOMORE YEAR

Lesson on Dealing with Mortality

Class 1: Biology Professor Lecture on Infectious Diseases.

Synopsis: Infectious diseases vary significantly, but have enough common characteristics to make them distinct and remarkable. For example, they strike suddenly and unexpectedly, and can affect otherwise healthy people, leading quickly to severe disability and death among some individuals while others recover spontaneously and completely. Although we now know more about the causes and treatment of infectious disease, that has not always been the case. This has led to panic, though with the advance of science, cures have often proven to be simple, safe, and effective, with preventives and medication fairly affordable. However, until science comes up with answers, human fear can cause panic. Examples discussed included the bubonic plague of the fourteenth century and the AIDS epidemic of the 1980s.

Class 2:

Out of Class Assignment: View the University of Glasgow's Special Collection's "Dancing with Death" exhibit online at http://special.lib.gla.ac.uk/exhibns/death/origins.html, which explores the "origins and development of the Dance of Death motif and its representation in graphic art;" and the Visual AIDS Exhibit at https://visualaids.org/gallery/detail/340, which examines "how artists living with HIV have treated AIDS in their work over the course of the epidemic, and how art has shaped the cultural and political response to HIV/AIDS."

(1) Write a paragraph reaction to each exhibit; (2) Draw a Dance of Death sketch; (3) Post three questions to the class—one dealing with the Glasgow Collection, one with the AIDS Exhibit, and one based on your thoughts on mortality.

In-Class Activities: Class discusses the parallels and contrasts between the motifs of medieval art and modern art around themes of death using questions posted by the students. Connections are made to the issues of fear and uncertainty, and insights from the lecture by the Biology professor are drawn upon. Students briefly share their artwork, explaining the reasoning behind what they drew. They receive input and critique from their classmates.

Class 3:

Out of Class Assignment: Students work with a member of the Art Department (either an upper-division peer mentor or a faculty member) who has agreed to help develop the student's art work. Using the feedback, the student revises the piece.

In-Class Activity: Students present their revised work to the class for comment and critique.

Class 4:

Out of Class Assignment: Write an essay considering what happens when medicine does not have the answers? How does the individual and society deal with the real possibility of death, painful, sudden, unpredictable? What are the lessons from our past? Does time and place matter—consider the gap in time and place between medieval society, the 1980s, and today—or are there some things that are just fundamental and transcendent?

In-Class Activity: Discussion focuses on the questions raised by the papers that students have been asked to write.

For now, the focus of the class has shifted. As changes were redefining life in the West, social development took a different path in Asia, Africa, and the Americas. Students are reminded of this as they examine the cultural developments of the Khan and Ming Dynasties in China, the Gupta Dynasty to the early Mughal Dynasty in India, the Aztec, Inca, and Mayan Dynasties in

Central and South America, and the Pueblo and Mississippian cultures of North America. In Africa, they learn about the renaissance of culture and economics centered on the Axum Empire, the Kingdom of Ghana, the Mali Empire, the Songhai Empire, the Ethiopian Empire, the Mossi Kingdoms, and the Benin Empire, which stood in sharp juxtaposition with the so-called European dark ages. Additionally, they explore the complex international system that linked Asia, the Middle East, East Africa, and northwest Europe before the sixteenth century. The instructor never seems to miss an opportunity to raise questions that ask them to draw contrasts and comparisons across cultures (*social organization*).

At the end of the semester, students are asked to attend a panel discussion with professors from the History, Philosophy, Religious Studies, Biology, Mathematics, Art, English, and Sociology Departments on something called *consilience*, or the unity of knowledge. They speak of the interconnection of their various branches of study, and students are asked to reflect back on the past sixteen weeks for evidence of the truth of what they are being told. Who would have thought, for example, how much biology would have influenced history, art, literature, and religion?

For some students—many, hopefully—a lightbulb goes on as they think about some of the other classes they have taken, and not just the three core courses so far. Over break, they may even tell their family and friends what they learned, which may pay off in future recruitment, a testimony to the power of word-of-mouth advertising. Certainly it should also help something every institution of higher learning is concerned with these days—retention.

Second Semester

This term students are signed up for *Global Encounters*, which is focused on the fifteenth through seventeenth centuries, when "the European synthesis born of the Middle Ages set in motion economic, political, and social changes that established the foundation for the Renaissance, the Reformation, overseas exploration, and the Scientific Revolution." They will be examining "the dramatic consequences of new or rediscovered ways of thinking on life in Europe, Asia, Africa, and the Americas." If they have bought into the ethos of the program, students should be anticipating an interesting semester.

In the first week, they are reminded of themes from freshman year, when the ideas from the Greeks and Romans influenced everything from understandings of *human nature* to aesthetics (*values*), and from politics to economics (*social organization*). Only now it is about a thousand years later, and there has been a shift in the balance of thinking in Western thought from the *faith* perspectives of the Middle Ages to the *reason* of the Renaissance, which ushered in a return to a focus on the classics.

Students are reminded of the forces that led to this transformation, for had it not been for the early stirrings of capitalism and nationalism (*social organization*), the Renaissance (*reason*) and Reformation (*faith*) would not have been possible. As in earlier classes, they are asked to compare this age with earlier periods, noting that although one or another theme may help define an era, the human experience is nuanced and complex.

Professors from the Political Science, Economics, Religious Studies, and Art Departments offer a panel presentation on the role of technology, politics, and economics on human understanding and representations of the Divine (*reason, social organization, values, human nature, faith*). Among other things, they discuss the rise of the so-called Protestant work ethic and the re-definition of religion in early modern Europe. Students are also asked to read Erik Erikson's psycho-biography *Young Man Luther* (*human nature*). Class discussion explores the way *faith*, fueled by the Reformation, was influenced by new technologies like the printing press, and with it, the role of the church and the laity in society and politics (*social organization, values*).

Their writing assignment at this point is interesting. Paralleling what they were asked to do with death motifs last semester, they examine several pieces of art and literature inspired by the *faith* of the Renaissance. With a bit of luck and advanced planning, some of the students in the program may have a role in Shakespeare's *A Midsummer Night's Dream*, which is being performed by the Theatre Department. It is something a few of them would never have thought of trying out for, had their advisors not encouraged them to take a "Fundamentals of Acting" class. Now, several members of the program are the "resident experts" as the class talks about Shakespeare and the play they have all been required to read and attend.

As the focus of discussion turns to the contrasts of *values* between what was produced in the Medieval and Renaissance periods, the differences between the two eras seem especially striking. The professor reminds the class that the differences are reflective of something they discussed last semester—that from the devastation of the bubonic plague would emerge a new world order.

As they study the political struggles that redefined national borders (*social organization*), students read Niccolò Machiavelli's *The Prince* and debate the implications of his arguments for the acquisition of overseas empire. This debate is revisited several times over the course of the second half of the semester as the interaction of Europe with the broader world is examined from a cross-cultural perspective.

Asian, African, and Native American cultures are discussed individually first, setting the stage for factors that will shape the nature and direction of encounters with the West. Put simply, *faith*, their rational constructs (*reason*), and their *values*, to say nothing of their military and economic might (*social organization*) and their environment (*nature*), determined how peaceful or violent the interactions ultimately became. It was no accident that China's isolationist attitudes and its economic and military might defined a controlled encounter with Europe, for example, while religious beliefs and biological weaknesses opened the Aztecs up to hostile takeover.

As the semester draws to a close, students are asked to consider the implications of the changes discussed in the course for the modern world. The Forensics Society hosts a debate that they are required to attend: "Should Columbus Day Still Be Celebrated?" The premise speaks directly to the costs and benefits of the Age of Exploration they have been discussing and debating in class.

The term ends with a presentation by members of the Physics Department on the ideas of Copernicus, Galileo, Newton, and Kepler. Students are reminded of the consilience talk they attended, since without the changes of the Renaissance and Reformation, and other topics that they have discussed this semester, everything that is the basis of science and technology—modern thinking, empirical analysis (*reason*), the understanding of the universe (*nature*) and humanity's place in it—would not be possible. Encouraged to see such connections, students are taught that this historical content is *relevant*!

TEXTBOX 6.4. INSIDE THE CLASSROOM: SECOND SEMESTER, SOPHOMORE YEAR

Lesson on Cultural Encounters

Note: Students have read and discussed Machiavelli's *The Prince* and have been given background on the competition for empire following the beginnings of Portuguese and Spanish overseas exploration, including the nature of imperial administration in the New World.

Class 1:

Out of Class Assignment: Read Hernan Cortés, Selected Letters from Mexico to Emperor Charles V; Selections from Bernal Díaz del Castillo, *Historia Verdadera de la Conquista de la Nueva España*.

Synopsis: Cortés recounted his army's experiences and explained his decisions, arguing that his actions enhanced the Emperor's power, wealth, and glory. Pointing to the savagery of the Aztecs, especially their use of human sacrifice, Cortés asserted the necessity of "civilizing" them by converting them to Christianity. Bernal Díaz was a soldier under Cortés.

The selections from his memoir focus on his impressions of Aztec culture and civilization, including its real accomplishments. For example, "And when we saw all those cities and villages built in the water, and other great towns on dry land, and that straight and level causeway leading to Mexico [i.e., Tenochtitlán], we were astounded. These great towns and cues [i.e., temples] and buildings rising from the water, all made of stone, seemed like an enchanted vision from the tale of Amadis."

Out of Class Assignment: (1) Write a paragraph reaction to each reading. (2) Post three questions to the class raised by the readings.

In-Class Activities: Students discuss Cortés's and Bernal Díaz's perspectives on Aztec culture using the questions they have submitted. The professor directs the conversation to the question, "What perspective is missing?" Students are asked to wrestle with the issue of ways to understand Native-American perspectives in light of the history of conquest.

Class 2:

Out of Class Assignment: Visit the website "The Conquest of Mexico," The American Historical Association, https://www.historians.org/teaching -and-learning/teaching-resources-for-historians/teaching-and-learning-in -the-digital-age/the-history-of-the-americas/the-conquest-of-mexico, and pay particular attention to the primary sources. Based on the primary sources, write an essay on the "Conquest of Mexico" from a strictly Native-American perspective.

In-Class Activities: Students talk about the nature of the sources that remain extant and about their frustration in trying to reconstruct a purely Native-American perspective of events from the historical record. This leads to a discussion of the role of culture in shaping historical narrative, understanding, and perspective.

Class 3:

Out of Class Assignment: Read selections from Bartolomé de las Casas, *A Short Account of the Destruction of the Indies.*

Synopsis: Las Casas wrote a description of reality that stood in sharp contrast to the perspectives of leaders like Cortés. A Dominican friar, Las Casas appealed to Charles V's sense of justice, morality, and Christianity. He wrote frankly about the exploitation and violence foisted on Native Americans by the Spanish, describing in often graphic detail the extensive torture, murder, and mutilation of the Indians, whom he called "innocent Sheep."

Out of Class Assignment: (1) Write a paragraph reaction to the reading. (2) Post three questions to the class raised by the reading.

In-Class Activities: Students discuss the implications of Las Casas's charges using the questions they have submitted. The professor raises the question of whether the Athenians were right when they told the Melians: "[T]he powerful exact what they can, and the weak grant what they must." After all, Machiavelli argued that power was the end game for the prince. Cortés sought to persuade Charles V that his actions against the Aztecs in essence were justified in Machiavellian terms, though it is doubtful he ever read *The Prince*. However, Las Casas believed otherwise. Reforms were implemented, including the New Laws of 1542, which abolished native slavery. Moreover, it is pointed out that Spanish cruelty was not completely at fault for the devastation of Native culture. As with the bubonic plague, there were natural forces that were beyond anyone's control. Native Americans lacked antibodies to many of the diseases carried by Europeans.

Class 4:

Out of Class Assignment: Write a paper addressing the question of whether the history of Spain's encounter with the Aztecs proved the Athenian assertion that the professor raised in class: Do "the powerful exact what they can, and the weak grant what they must"?

In-Class Activities: Students discuss their essays, which leads to exploration of the implications of the issues for the larger question of whether virtue matters, which was at the heart of the Melian Dialogue discussion first semester freshman year, from which this essay prompt came.

Chapter Seven

To Graduation and Beyond

A Student's-Eye View Continued

Back on campus, Juniors probably cannot believe that half their college career is over. With summer gone, they realize that they will need to start thinking about the future a little more seriously. But there is still time. Right now, it is about reconnecting with old friends, talking about what happened over the last few months, and unpacking. Oh yeah, and calling home.

JUNIOR YEAR

First Semester

The core course this term is *Enlightenment and Revolution*, which promises to "consider the ideas of selected Enlightenment thinkers whose work in political theory, moral philosophy, and economics transformed Western, and eventually global, ways of thinking." Students will also be examining "the eighteenth- and early nineteenth-century revolutions that ushered in the beginnings of modern politics, economics, and society."

On the first day, the professor tells the class that what they will be studying this semester sets in motion forces that moved society toward modernity, transforming humanity's understanding of itself (*human nature*), of how it should organize its governments, societies, and economies (*social organization*), and how that affected the definition of everything from justice to beauty (*values*). He points out that despite the overwhelming emphasis placed on *reason* by Enlightenment thinkers and the educated elite of the period, *faith* and tradition persisted.

Coexisting with and adapting to the rise of rationalism, these older ways of knowing worked in tandem with the rediscovery of reason to usher in new ways of understanding and of conceptualizing and organizing society (*social organization*). The first week then involves a discussion of how these forces have worked in past societies to inform their development and evolution, laying the basis for comparisons with what will be examined this semester.

It does not take long to see why the course is introduced in this way. The seventeenth and eighteenth centuries marked the emergence of a new political and intellectual order in the West. Over the next few weeks, students read and discuss the works of Thomas Hobbes, John Locke, Jean Jacques Rousseau, and Adam Smith as examples of the logic of authoritarianism, liberalism, socialism, and capitalism, respectively (*reason, human nature, social organization*).

They then read some works from Immanuel Kant, who sought to unite reason with experience and thereby move beyond what he believed were the failures of traditional philosophy and metaphysics (*reason, human nature*). This is followed by David Hume, who proposed to create a total naturalistic "science of man" that examined the psychological basis of *human nature* (*nature, reason*). Finally, they study Rene Descartes, who emphasized the use of reason to develop the natural sciences (*nature, reason*).

Students are asked to reflect on the fact that the Enlightenment, borrowing from breakthroughs in science, helped to focus on age-old questions that the Ancient Greeks and Romans had wrestled with, and in the process shaped and defined modern ways of knowing. The thinkers they are studying dealt with the very nature of humanity (*human nature*)—our inherent goodness or intractability (*values*)—how we know (*reason*), and the best means of governing ourselves (*social organization*).

In class, students are asked to reflect on the influences of these new ways of thought on Western aesthetics (*values*). A professor from the Art Department gives a lecture on the neoclassical art and architecture of the seventeenth and eighteenth centuries. The talk explains Greek and Roman influences, which seem obvious enough in the art and architecture. However, as the discussion afterward makes clear, there is a symmetry between the ideas informing the art of the period and what was preoccupying its philosophers.

In the next class, another guest lecturer, this time from the Music Department, speaks about Johann Sebastian Bach and Wolfgang Amadeus Mozart, pointing out how Bach's work had a mathematical precision, intellectual depth, technical command, and artistic beauty, while Mozart's music spanned the gambit from the light and graceful to the dark and passionate. Both, she notes, reflected influences in their lives, and just as significantly, shaped the future of Western music (*values*).

Students are asked to attend a recital of selected works by Bach and Mozart performed by students in the music program and to write a reflective piece on the experience. They may never have willingly gone to such a concert before, but having attended and understood something about what they are hearing, they may begin to appreciate it, even if it still might not be what they choose to load to their iTunes playlist.

During the second half of the semester, they focus on the tension that existed between the rationalism of the Enlightenment (*reason*) and the continuing importance of *faith*. They consider the role of the Reformation in the development of the Atlantic world, inspiring revolutions in the Netherlands and England, encouraging migration to the New World by Pilgrims and Puritans, and fostering the First Great Awakening. Studying the Dutch, English, American, French, Haitian, and Latin American revolutions, they are asked to consider the foundational documents of each and the role that culture played in shaping how the ideals of democracy (*values*) were operationalized across time and place (*social organization*).

TEXTBOX 7.1. INSIDE THE CLASSROOM: FIRST SEMESTER, JUNIOR YEAR

Lesson on Balancing Individual Rights and the Common Good

Note: Students have been given background on the Dutch and English revolutions; have studied the period of American colonization, including the Mayflower Compact; know the details of the American Revolution and its immediate aftermath; and have studied the ideas of John Locke, Thomas Hobbes, and Jean-Jacques Rousseau prior to this lesson.

Class 1:

Out of Class Assignment: Read the United States Articles of Confederation; United States Constitution; United States Bill of Rights; *Federalist Papers* 6, 7, 8, 9, 10, 16, 17, 18, 19, 20, 51; *Anti-Federalist Papers* 1, 7, 9, 11, 13, 17, 22, 26, 37, 41–43.

Synopsis: The Articles of Confederation established an agreement between the several states, severely limiting the power of the federal government. The Constitution set up an alternative to that system, which established the system under which the United States still operates, with three branches of government and checks and balances on power. The Bill of Rights, or first ten amendments to the Constitution, guarantee the rights to which citizens are entitled. The *Federalist Papers* provide the rationale for the Constitution as a means by which government can both be functional and serve the common good, and still preserve individual liberty. The *Anti-Federalist Papers* raise objections to the possible abuses of power that a strong central government poses, not the least of which because of an executive branch.

Out of Class Assignment: (1) Write a reaction paper to the *Federalist* and *Anti-Federalist Papers*, paying particular attention to their implications not only for the strengths and weaknesses of the Articles of Confederation, Constitution, and Bill of Rights at the time that they were written, but also for today, given contemporary arguments about the size and purpose of government. (2) Post three questions to the class raised by the readings.

In-Class Activities: Students discuss the questions they have submitted. The professor focuses the conversation on the issue, "How much government is enough government or too much government?" As the class winds down, students take the "World's Smallest Political Quiz" (https://www.theadvocates.org/quiz/?gclid=EAIaIQobChMIi4_h4NPD4A IVAVgNCh1qyg2CEAAYASAAEgKcFfD_BwE).

Class 2:

Out of Class Assignment: Revise the Response Essay in light of the class discussion and the political quiz.

In-Class Activities: Students discuss the revisions to their essays and why they made them. They reflect on the accuracy of the "World's Shortest Political Quiz" and then talk more fully about the question posed in the previous class about how much government is enough or too much. Based on the rough division of class opinion, the class is split up between Federalists and Anti-Federalists. Depending on class size, thirteen "delegations" are created, one for each of the states. In the time remaining, students are allowed to talk in groups to begin planning how they will make their case in a Mock Constitutional Convention during the next class.

Class 3:

Out of Class Assignment: Groups continue to meet to discuss what their positions will be.

In-Class Activities: The class stages a Mock Constitutional Convention, with the professor serving as president of the convention. Time is allotted toward the end of the convention to debrief the exercise and extrapolate major lessons.

Class 4:

Out of Class Assignment: Revise the Response Essay a final time in light of the previous three classes.

In-Class Activities: Students discuss their essays and the major "take aways" from their experience with the lesson. In the course of the discussion, the professor posits a new variable: To what extent does culture or time period matter? What needs did Americans face in the eighteenth century? What about now? How did that compare with those of the Dutch or the English? Is Democracy a "cure-all?" Students are asked to keep these questions in mind, since they will be studying the French, Haitian, and Latin American revolutions next.

The professor leaves the class with a question at the end of the semester: "Which is more important—culture or ideas? If there is such a thing as universal human rights—those natural laws and truths that transcend time and place—then that explains the impulse of freedom manifested in the revolutions we have examined and the struggle for liberty you will be studying in the next three semesters of the program. However, why are there such vast differences in their operationalization? What role does culture play in shaping human experience?"

These are interesting things to think about. For some of the students, that may happen as they study abroad during the winter term between semesters. They'll spend three and a half weeks in Italy, visiting sites from Ancient Rome to the Renaissance. This is a nice recap of everything they have covered in the core thus far. Plus, it is Italy!

Second Semester

This semester's offering is *Reflections of Modernity*, which "focuses on the transformation of the Western political, economic, and cultural landscape." According to the course description, "As science, technology, and industrialization redefined life, people sought meaning and understanding in a variety of ways, both traditional and modern. Against this backdrop, the realities of power and economics continued to shape class, race, and gender relations." As veterans of the program, students can almost anticipate some of the issues. Certainly, the question that their professor left them with at the end of the last term gives them some ways to frame what is probably in store.

The course begins by examining the advances made by science in the nineteenth century. Students read excerpts from Charles Darwin's *On the Origin of Species*; John Dalton's *Memoir of John Dalton*, Georg Ohm's *The Galvanic Circuit Investigated Mathematically*, and Michael Faraday's *On the Various Forces of Nature*. They also attend a symposium on scientific thinking featuring members of the Biology, Chemistry, and Physics Departments (*nature, reason*).

The class then examines the practical implications of scientific breakthroughs for technology and the growth of industry. They discuss the industrial revolution and the effects of innovation, ranging from the cotton gin to steam power to the factory (*social organization*). The class then focuses on the ways in which science reinterpreted the physical and natural world (*reason, nature*), which called into question not only humanity's place in the universe but the very essence of what it means to be human (*human nature, values*).

This leads to an examination of the responses to these issues. In the second third of the term, students examine the Second Great Awakening (*faith*) in the United States, read several works from the Romantic literary movement, including the poems of John Keats and Lord Byron, and excerpts from Mary Shelly's *Frankenstein*. They explore the works of Ralph Waldo Emerson and Henry David Thoreau, as well as the concepts of idealism represented by Georg Hegel and Arthur Schopenhauer, utilitarianism by Jeremy Bentham and John Stuart Mill, and positivism by Auguste Comte. The discussions focus on familiar issues: *nature, human nature, reason, social organization*, and *values*.

As this part of the course draws to a close, students are reminded again about the question their professor posed last semester. In fact, their instructor raises it again now. "Think about something," he says. "What does what we have been talking about suggest about the effects of culture on how the supposedly universal truths of the Enlightenment are implemented?"

And with that, students begin examining a whole set of different issues that put that question to the test. They read works that advocate women's equality, including Mary Wollstonecraft's *A Vindication of the Rights of Woman*; that condemn slavery, including selections from William Lloyd Garrison's *The Liberator*, Frederick Douglass's *Narrative of the Life of Frederick Douglass*, and Solomon Northup's *Twelve Years a Slave*; and that analyze the influence of industrial capitalism, including selections by Karl Marx and Frederick Engels (*human nature, social organization, values*).

Lesson on Liberty

Note: Students have read and discussed John Stuart Mill's *On Liberty* and have a background on the realities of slavery in the American South and the legal status of women in the United States and England during the period.

Class 1:

Out of Class Assignment: Read Selections from Frederick Douglass's *Narrative of the Life of Frederick Douglass and* **Solomon** Northup's *Twelve Years a Slave.*

Synopsis: The selections from Douglass's *Narrative* focus on his treatment as a slave and his growing desire for freedom and eventual escape. Northup's story was different. Born free in 1808 in Minerva, New York, he had an interesting life until he was tricked into taking a job with a circus. In short order, he found himself drugged in the nation's capital, then sold south into slavery. The next twelve years were a succession of cruelties, witnessed and experienced.

Out of Class Assignment: (1) Write a paragraph reaction to each reading. (2) Post three questions to the class raised by the readings.

In-Class Activities: Students discuss the readings using the questions they have submitted. The professor raises the question of how one operationalizes liberty and reminds students of John Stuart Mill's *On Liberty* criteria. According to Mill, "the only purpose for which power can be rightfully exercised over any member of a civilized community, against his will, is to prevent harm to others." Under this criteria, slavery makes no sense. Nor does it under the universal ideals of the Enlightenment or of Judeo-Christian ethics. Students are reminded that this was also the time of the Second Great Awakening. Again, Mill is raised. By his criteria, humans have three basic rights: (1) freedom of thought and emotion; (2) freedom to pursue tastes; and (3) freedom to unite so long as the members are of age, are not forced, and no harm is done. Given this, students are reminded that Mill advocated for government noninterference in all aspects of life, including the economy. Finally, students are referred back to "The World's Smallest Political Quiz" and talk about the difficulty of balancing personal and economic issues. The question is posed—why did slavery exist? The implications of that question are discussed in terms of economic and personal rights and the inevitability of factionalism, and the debate over the US Constitution is revisited.

Class 2:

Out of Class Assignment: Read selections from William Lloyd Garrison's *The Liberator*, Mary Wollstonecraft's *A Vindication of the Rights of Woman*, Sojourner Truth's *Speeches*, and *The Declaration of the Seneca Falls Convention*.

Synopsis: Garrison's *Liberator* was the mouthpiece for the abolitionist movement, and then the women's rights movement. The selections highlight the arguments for both movements as they evolved together. Wollstonecraft argued that society rested on the equal education and, by extension, treatment of both sexes. As she put it, "if [woman] be not prepared by education to become the companion of man, she will stop the progress of knowledge and virtue; for truth must be common to all." Further, Wollstonecraft contended that education involved "an exercise of the understanding as is best calculated to strengthen the body and form the heart. Or, in other words, to enable the individual to attach such habits of virtue as will render it independent." The women who gathered at Seneca Falls, New York, in 1848 had in many cases begun their activism in the abolition movement. In the *Declaration*, they put forth their reasons for "assum[ing] among the people of the earth a position different from that which they have hitherto occupied, but one to which the laws of nature and of nature's God entitle them." Sojourner Truth's *Speeches* address her views as an abolitionist and as a feminist. Speaking plainly and clearly as an African-American woman and a former slave, she saw that the issues crossed gender, class, and racial lines, or as she put it, "Well, children, where there is so much racket there must be something out of kilter. I think that 'twixt the negroes of the South and the women at the North, all talking about rights, the white men will be in a fix pretty soon. But what's all this here talking about?"

Out of Class Assignment: (1) Write a paragraph reaction to each reading. (2) Post three questions to the class raised by the readings.

In-Class Activities: Students discuss the readings using the questions they have submitted. The conversation again focuses on the implications of Mill and the issue of balancing economic and personal rights. The question is raised as to how one defines virtue, since Wollstonecraft argued that the purpose of education for women as for men was the teaching of virtue. If equality and the betterment of society means expanding access to the best of what society has to offer, then clearly this is something to which excluded groups in a free society should have access. The professor points out the lessons of the past dating back to Socrates, then reminds the class what Mill said about the three basic freedoms. Are they valid? Do they align with the demand in *The Declaration of the Seneca Falls Convention?* What obstacles do women and African Americans face in society? Is it enough for liberty to be implemented along the model suggested by Mill?

Class 3:

Out of Class Assignment: Write a draft of an essay *On Liberty* taking into account the readings and discussions of the last two classes.

In-Class Activities: Students are organized into small editorial groups during which they read and critique each other's essays. The professor circulates among the groups, providing feedback and assistance.

Class 4:

Out of Class Assignment: Revise essay *On Liberty* based on peer and faculty input.

In-Class Activities: Students discuss their *On Liberty* essays, exploring the issues of *nature, human nature, values, faith,* and *reason* for *social organization,* all the themes of the liberal arts core.

Students examine what happened as a result of these ideas by studying the struggle for women's rights in the United States and England in the nineteenth century, the American Civil War, and the European revolutions of 1848 (*social organization*). The comparisons raise interesting issues, many of which have contemporary ramifications. To drive that point home, the professor reminds the class of the title of the course: *Reflections of Modernity.*

SENIOR YEAR

As fall arrives, it is probably difficult for some seniors to believe that they will be graduating this year. Where did the time go? They need to start thinking about looking for a job. Maybe graduate school is a good idea. Then

again, they do have those student loans. These are all things to think about
. . . but later.

First Semester

Right now they are signed up for *Costs and Consequences of Modernism*,
a class that says it will look at not only how "technology and science continued to redefine everything from ways of thinking and understanding to
how people interacted," but how "old perspectives and national rivalries
and aspirations informed the backdrop against which change unfolded." It
is also going to consider how "industrialization made production of new
weaponry possible," turning "the twentieth century into the most deadly in
human history."

Students will be asked to "consider the resulting irony that as humans
gained more control and understanding of the universe, they found the ultimate meaning and purpose of life more elusive." Given their own feelings
about the future, the course seems tuned in to the current frame of mind of
many in the class.

The professor starts by asking students to consider how change in the
Western world transformed the political, economic, and cultural landscape
(*social organization*) and how international trade brought the world closer
than it had ever been. They assess the costs and consequences of these developments both at home and abroad and are reminded that in the *Reflections of
Modernity* class, they already witnessed how the *values* of capitalism, liberalism, and *faith* were often at odds with one another.

In the first month of the class, students study existentialism, pragmatism,
and idealism, reading, respectively, selections from the works of Friedrich
Nietzsche, Søren Kierkegaard, William James, Walt Whitman, and Mark
Twain. They then are introduced to Sigmund Freud's *Psychopathology of
Everyday Life*. Discussions focus on the implications of these works for an
understanding of *human nature, nature*, and *values*.

A professor from the Psychology Department gives a guest lecture on
James and Freud (*reason, human nature*). In the following class, a member
of the English faculty leads a discussion on Whitman's *Leaves of Grass* (*values*). In the next class, one of the art professors offers a presentation on the
artistic movements and styles that came into vogue between 1870 and 1930,
including impressionism, postimpressionism, fauvism, expressionism, abstract, cubism, futurism, suprematism, constructivism, and de Stijl (*values*).

Students learn how these styles were either expressions of or reactions to
modernism, and how they spoke to many of the issues confronting the period
that were addressed by the philosophers and writers they have been discuss-

ing. They are then asked to write an essay contrasting the ways of understanding represented by these philosophical, literary, and artistic expressions with those of the Ancient Greeks and the Enlightenment.

The focus of the course then shifts to the real-world implications of the changes transforming society. The class examines the international implications of the causes of these new perspectives by considering how Europeans and Americans wrestled with the consequences of unbridled industrialization and imperialism (*social organization*). Sometimes the ideals of human rights (*values*) born of the Enlightenment (*reason*) and the belief in the brotherhood of humanity inspired by Christianity (*faith*) served as a social conscience that inspired reform.

At other times, however, pseudoscience (*reason*) combined with evangelical zeal (*faith*) to rationalize exploitation. Students read and debate the ideas of Walter Rauschenbusch and Herbert Spencer, then examine the realities of industrialization, urbanization, and the economic distribution of wealth in the late nineteenth and early twentieth centuries.

Attention next turns to international relations, in particular late nineteenth- and early twentieth-century imperialism. The class reads excerpts from Rudyard Kipling's "Gunga Din" and his "White Man's Burden," Joseph Conrad's *Heart of Darkness,* and Swami Vivekananda's *Speeches in Chicago.* Additionally, they examine the imperialist experience of selected nations in Asia, Africa, and Latin America, whose responses were shaped by their unique situations (*social organization*), which included their *faith* and *values*.

Students are asked to think about why, despite their diversity of response—ranging from accommodation and compromise to resistance—each society in some way sought to do what the Qing Dynasty of China attempted to do by pursuing a policy premised on the logic of "east for essence, west for practical use" (*social organization, values*). "It is a difficult balancing act," their professor points out, "even today." With that, the class examines current events in light of their historical context.

Because all of these issues were played out against the backdrop of continued scientific advancements (*reason*) that redefined humanity's understanding of *nature*, students are required to attend a lecture presented by the Physics Department on "The Fundamentals of Quantum Physics." Since most are not scientists, the talk is designed for a lay audience. The themes are fairly straightforward. Physics, because of Albert Einstein, Max Planck, Erwin Schrödinger, and Georges Lemaître, changed everything.

Just how important those changes were is the subject of the next class discussion, where students are asked to reflect on how *this* scientific revolution was probably even more significant than the one in the seventeenth century, though it would not have been possible if the first one had not occurred. They are reminded yet again about consilience and the importance of the interconnection of ideas across time, a central focus of the program.

The implications of this are reinforced when the class is asked to consider the first forty-five years of the twentieth century. Science and technology were changing the way the world understood itself (*values, social organization*) and what humans could do, but it did not change some basic issues involving justice, fairness, and virtue, the things people like Socrates were talking about some 2,500 years ago.

With that as the baseline for discussion, students spend the last part of the semester studying World War I, the Russian Revolution, the Great Depression, and World War II. They examine some of the foundational documents surrounding those events, including excerpts from Woodrow Wilson, Franklin Roosevelt, and Herbert Hoover's speeches, V. I. Lenin's *State and Revolution*, Adolf Hitler's *Mein Kampf*, and the Atlantic Charter (*social organization, human nature, values*). They also study the consequences of these events by reading passages from Erich Remarque's *All Quiet on the Western Front*, John Steinbeck's *The Grapes of Wrath*, Elie Wiesel's *Night*, and John Hershey's *Hiroshima* (*social organization, human nature, values*).

**TEXTBOX 7.3. INSIDE THE CLASSROOM:
FIRST SEMESTER, SENIOR YEAR**

Lesson on War and Peace in the Modern Era

Note: Students have studied the origins of World War I and its aftermath, examined the rise of Bolshevism in Russia and the global Great Depression, and discussed the Second World War.

Class 1:

Out of Class Assignment: Read selections from Erich Remarque, *All Quiet on the Western Front*, Elie Wiesel's *Night*, John Hershey's *Hiroshima*, Woodrow Wilson's "Fourteen Points Speech," the Atlantic Charter, and the United Nations Charter.

Synopsis: Remarque described the horrors of modern war during World War I. Wiesel told of his experience at the Nazi concentration camps at Auschwitz and Buchenwald. Hershey recounted the lives of six survivors of the atomic bomb from 1945 to 1984. Wilson's Fourteen Points, the Atlantic Charter, and the United Nations Charter were responses to the cost of war in the modern era.

Out of Class Assignment: (1) Write a reaction paper considering the following—Do justice and virtue matter? If you recall, it is a theme you addressed in freshman year and over the course of the program, including when we discussed the ideas of Machiavelli and the perspective of Thomas Hobbes. In light of these readings and what you have learned about the first forty-five years of the twentieth century, what do you think and why? (2) Post three questions to the class raised by the readings.

In-Class Activities: Students discuss the questions they have submitted. The professor focuses the conversation on their essays. There is much discussion about the "lessons of history" and their implications in the modern era. As a closing thought, the professor asks students to think what they would do if they were either Woodrow Wilson, Franklin Roosevelt, or Winston Churchill and were seeking to create a "New World Order" based on the lessons of history.

Class 2:

Out of Class Assignment: Write a "White Paper" outlining your plan for world peace based on the historical lessons you have learned since freshman year. What is there about *nature, human nature, faith, reason, values,* and *social organization* that need to be considered in framing a viable path forward?

In-Class Activities: Students discuss their "White Papers" in small groups and then present their group findings to the class. The class talks about and critiques the ideas presented.

Class 3:

Out of Class Assignment: Groups take the comments and critiques and develop a revised group "White Paper" to be presented in class.

In-Class Activities: The groups present their revised "White Papers," which stimulates a discussion on the question of what factors shape the issues of war and peace in the modern era, how they are unique to this period, and to what extent they speak to something fundamental about human nature.

Class 4:

Out of Class Assignment: Each student revises his or her reaction paper on the question, Do justice and virtue matter?

In-Class Activities: Students discuss their essays. Class focuses on the implications of the issues raised by the discussion and the semester and the themes of the program. Specifically they consider the dialectic between the illusion of control offered by scientific understanding and technological innovation, and the enduring human struggle for meaning.

As the semester draws to an end, students are asked to consider one of the great ironies born of this period. To wit: Why is it that the more control of the physical environment and understanding of the universe (*nature*) humans have acquired, the more elusive the ultimate meaning and purpose of life (*values*) seem to have become? The professor makes a point to remind the class that these issues have kept coming up for a reason, and that reason is why they have been taking the courses in the program.

Second Semester

The final class in the core is *Ideology, Technology, and Global Challenges*, which will bring the story current. According to the course description,

> The continuing search for meaning has occurred in the shadow of weapons of mass destruction, instantaneous communication, and economic and environmental challenges. In many ways, the modern era has been a combination of constancy and change. As technology continues to push out the envelope of what is possible, the fundamental concerns of humanity continue to demand answers. This will be the central focus of discussion in this course.

Those last two sentences by now should ring true, especially given the connections that *purposely* have been made between the topics the students have examined since freshman year.

During the first third of the semester, the focus is on the conflict of *values* and *social organization* represented by the Cold War between the United States and Soviet Union, including the overlay of *faith* and materialism (or as the Russians would have it, the rationalism [*reason*] of dialectic materialism) that informed each side's critique of the other. The insanity of mutual assured destruction drove the superpowers to seek influence in a developing world that found itself emerging from the shadow of imperialism. Examining the foundational issues and documents of superpower foreign policy, the class turns its attention to the ideas emerging in the so-called Third World, reading selections from Mohandas Gandhi, Ho Chi Minh, Sukarno, and Jawaharlal Nehru.

As in the fall semester, students are asked to deal with how situations within emerging states (*social organization*) informed how they approached the struggle between the United States and Soviet Union. In what is by now a familiar lesson, they are reminded of the importance of culture and history. India, for example, turned to *faith* and the *values* of nonviolent resistance. China and Vietnam, on the other hand, adapted Marxist-Leninist ideas (*reason*) to make sense of their *social organization*.

Discussion focuses on the fact that, as in earlier times, larger social and political movements influenced the work of writers, artists, and musicians and the search for meaning (*values*). In this period, they gave birth to such developments as the beat movement, rock and roll, and abstract expressionism. Students read selections from Jack Kerouac and Allen Ginsberg, then attend a lecture by a member of the Art Department on abstract expressionism, pop art, op-art, and minimalism.

The Music Department then hosts a folk and rock revival of music from the 1950s and 1960s. Finally, the class is given a choice of reading Joseph Heller's *Catch-22* or Kurt Vonnegut's *Slaughterhouse-Five*. Discussion focuses on the nature of these various responses to the realities of war, genocide, and mutual assured destruction, and the continuing disconnect between the ideals of human rights (*values*) born of the Enlightenment (*reason*) and the demands of economic inequality that fostered racism, classcism, and sexism (*social organization*) during the Cold War.

The course then explores the ways that societies themselves dealt with these same paradoxes. Students read the words of Martin Luther King, who went to Washington in 1963 to "cash the check" written by the American Founding Fathers, and of Nelson Mandela, who declared his willingness to die for freedom. They also study the works of Betty Friedan, who gave voice to the modern American feminist movement, and Chandra Talpade Mohanty, who wrote of feminism in the developing world.

All of these works speak to issues of *human nature*, *values*, and *social organization*, as in earlier times, but in some cases, they also raise issues of *faith*, as with Martin Luther King and liberation theology, which gained currency in the 1970s. Students are asked to write a reflective essay on the historical lessons of social conscience.

As they study the end of the Cold War and the rise of terrorism, they read the ideas of Francis Fukuyama, who argued in the late 1980s and early 1990s that the last four hundred years marked the "triumph of the Western Idea"—in essence, the ideals embodied by the Enlightenment. The professor asks, "Given the struggles for freedom and the ideals espoused, especially since the end of World War II, was he right?"

It is a good question, but one that cannot be easily answered, as discussion in class makes clear. Yes, the close of the Cold War signaled the apparent victory of democracy and capitalism in some parts of the world, but the realities in Third and Fourth World nations, specifically economic and political instability (*social organization*), spawned terrorism elsewhere. Meanwhile environmental issues like global warming (*nature*) threatened the future of the planet in ways that people who lived through the days of mutual assured destruction could never have imagined. Additionally, systemic issues of poverty and racism (*social organization*), especially in the United States, have not been fully confronted despite the ideals of freedom and equality espoused in the West since the Enlightenment.

All this when the information superhighway and internet are making communication and cooperation easier, redefining how people interact (*social organization*), and changing the paradigms of human understanding (*reason*). These trends are at least in part driven by global capitalism (*social organization*) and have spawned a backlash to its evils, real or imagined, by *faith*-based fundamentalists of all stripes. A symposium on these issues brings together members of the International Relations, Environmental Studies, Economics, and Computer Science Departments to talk about present and future trends.

This is the world the graduating class will inherit. And that is the question they are asked to ponder in their final essay for the class: If past is prologue and the liberal arts core has done its job, what lessons are there from what you have learned as you face the future?

TEXTBOX 7.4. INSIDE THE CLASSROOM: SECOND SEMESTER, SENIOR YEAR

Lesson on Life in the Post-Modern Now

Class 1: (Note: Occurs early in the semester)

In-Class Activities: Professor lists the six program themes. Students are asked to brainstorm the current problems confronting society and place them under the appropriate themes. A survey is taken of the different majors in the class. Students decide which current issues they wish to tackle over the course of the semester and then organize themselves into task forces based on interest and expertise.

Class 2: (Note: Occurs about mid-semester)

Out of Class Assignment: Task force groups prepare detailed literature reviews. These are given to the professor and made available to the class. Each review is also provided to another group for peer critique. The critique is submitted in writing to the group and the professor, and is made available to the class.

In-Class Activities: Literature reviews are presented in a professional conference format, followed by peer review comments, and questions.

Class 3: (Note: Occurs toward the end of the semester)

Out of Class Assignment: Task force groups prepare a report detailing the issue, possible solutions, and recommendations. These are given to the professor and made available to the class. Each report is also provided to another group for peer critique. The critique is submitted in writing to the group and the professor, and is made available to the class.

In-Class Activities: Reports are presented in a professional conference format, followed by peer review comments, and questions.

PREPARING FOR LIFE, NOT A CAREER

So these students graduate and get that coveted degree. What next? Statistics vary, but the consensus suggests that they will have five to seven careers (of course, the definition of "career" varies and affects that number) and upward of fifteen jobs during their lifetimes.[1] The reason for such fluidity varies. Today's students want different things out of life than previous generations. They see the world differently. Given the rapidity with which the world keeps changing, it is fair to say that when they hit middle age, some careers they may be interested in did not exist when they graduated from college. How then could they have been trained for them?

It is possible that these students will be involved in the development of those careers, or that ancillary developments in areas unrelated to what they were trained to do will affect how they do their jobs in the future. At the end of their last semester in the program, they learned that there actually was a time shortly before they were born when the internet did not exist. Now it permeates every aspect of life. Put another way, as management expert Steve Denning says, "Everyone [today] accepts careers are no longer linear."[2]

So how does one prepare for such a reality? According to Guy Berger, an economist for LinkedIn, "The best advice I can give anyone is to think about acquiring skills and knowledge that can easily be transferred from one place to another."[3] Or in other words, get a liberal arts education that teaches one how to think critically by developing analytical skills through writing, speaking, and research, while wrestling with enduring human issues. If a student graduates with an understanding of the nature of the world they live in and the people with whom they share it, if they have the ability to reason and to communicate, they have a set of skills and a knowledge base that is transferable to any job or career, and beyond that, to life outside what they choose to do to earn their daily bread.

Chapter Eight

Beyond Platitudes
Remembering What It Is All About

Was the preceding four-year journey through the Liberal Arts Core romanticized and idealized? Of course. However, it was to make a point. A new old way of thinking about what must be done is necessary to meet the needs of students, and those needs can realistically be achieved even if only a small portion of what was outlined in the preceding two chapters occurred. Indeed, it would serve them far better than what most of them are getting now, and for the long haul, given the challenges of the future.

The point is to focus on the ultimate objective—the reason colleges and universities exist: to provide the best education possible to their students. If that is done, effective ways to build bridges across disciplines can be found that complement and enhance what each instructor and departmental program is doing to meet the needs of the young people they are there to serve. In doing so, they will fulfill their school's true institutional mission.

Indeed, the Radical Proposal, or a program like it, could afford a means of encouraging collegiality and cross-disciplinary cooperation. Instead of pitting area against area in a free-for-all competition for students that may be culled from the current general education offerings or distribution requirements, institutional cooperation could create unity of purpose and focus. And this is far better than abandoning the field completely, as has occurred at some institutions that continue to pare down their liberal arts requirements in the misbegotten notion that STEM, or perhaps STEAM, is the future or the salvation. A resurgence of the liberal arts is the key to *meaningful* institutional branding; *genuine, value-added* education; and truly *effective, positive* change.

Yes, the ideas in this book buck a trend. That is what makes them radical. But given that the trend is reflective of lemmings jumping off a cliff, maybe that is a good thing. The future does not lie in blindly following the pack, but in charting a new course. To follow the insane to their doom does not serve anyone. To understand the degree to which the infection has come to define administration logic, one need only examine the frequency with which institutions gut liberal arts majors and the rationale used to justify the wholesale closure of programs like history, English, philosophy, political science, sociology, and languages.

The case of the University of Wisconsin–Stevens Point, which announced draconian closures affecting thirteen liberal arts majors in March 2018, serves as an excellent case study. According to its provost, Greg Summers, the move was just a matter of "accept[ing] the need for change and confront[ing] the financial issues currently facing the institution . . . [while] creat[ing] a new identity."[1] That new identity somehow, according to the school's website, still involved a commitment

> to ensuring every student who graduates from UW–Stevens Point is thoroughly grounded in the liberal arts, as well as prepared for a successful career path. It is critical our students learn to communicate well, solve problems, think critically and creatively, be analytical and innovative, and work well in teams. This is the value of earning a bachelor's degree.[2]

The illogic of cutting programs in the liberal arts while asserting a commitment to programs grounded in their principles suggests just how far higher education has strayed from understanding the nature of what is at the heart of a liberal arts education. Without understanding the *longue durée*, people cannot grasp the consilience of human knowledge that is at the heart of the liberal arts, to which humanity is heir, and of which members of the academy are supposed to be trustees for future generations. In point of fact, humans become incapable of truly understanding anything. As such, they become Sophists, willing to traffic not in truth but in whatever the market will bear.

That is what institutions obsessed with their "brand" or creating a "new identity" are doing. How little things have changed since Ancient Greece. If Socrates were around, he might well inquire of today's parents, as he did of Callias, who "spent a world of money" for the education of his two sons, what their tuition dollars were going for. Like "Happy . . . Evenus," who collected his "modest fee" on the conceit that he knew things he did not,[3] educators would not have to keep reinventing themselves if they remembered the truths that the liberal arts have taught in the first place, one of which is humility. But that requires a willingness to take a broader look at the historical and cultural record, which involves *long-term thinking*, not short-term reaction.

Eventually, the market will win out, and quality education will triumph. The problem is not the failure of the liberal arts. It is the failure of the *practitioners* of the liberal arts to uphold and defend the standards of the liberal arts. Students and parents will not pay for shabby education or second-rate inquiry substituting for genuine intellectual inquiry and the pursuit of knowledge. They will not long be fooled by the amenities of campus life without the substance of academic rigor.

Vocational and online education will continue to have devotees, but those students seeking out education at high-priced brick and mortar institutions are going to want more than short-term fixes. The lesson is not that difficult to grasp. There is a reason Socrates and Plato are studied instead of Evenus, 2,500 years after they lived.

THE CHALLENGES OF LIVING IN A GLOBALIZED WORLD

In some sense, the liberal arts have fallen victim to what sociologist James Davison Hunter called the "culture wars." But it is those "culture wars," and the challenges of living in a globalized post–Cold War world, that are reminders of the liberal arts' continued relevancy. Hunter explored the domestic ramifications in a book by the same title published in 1991.[4] Its international dimensions were examined by two American political scientists, Samuel P. Huntington and Benjamin R. Barber, in two seminal studies that came out in 1996, *The Clash of Civilizations and the Remaking of World Order*[5] and *Jihad V. McWorld: How Globalism and Tribalism Are Reshaping the World*,[6] respectively.

All of these scholars in some way spoke to the fundamental flaw undergirding the idea that a New World Order, based on a consensus about the validity of the "Western idea," was possible. The latter argument was something that had been posited by Francis Fukuyama as the Cold War was drawing to close.

In 1989, Fukuyama argued that trends seemed to suggest that "something very fundamental has happened in world history." In particular, "the triumph of the West, of the Western *idea*," was evident everywhere. With the passing of Marxism-Leninism and the growing "'Common Marketization' of international relations," the beginning of the end of history was at hand. Although international conflict would not disappear completely, because the world would for a time be divided between those in the historical and the posthistorical phases of development, major conflicts between large states were "passing from the scene."[7]

Domestically, there have been few signs of that consensus. As Hunter pointed out, "The Enlightenment *philosophes* long ago predicted that, as societies advanced, modern individuals would outgrow their need for the comfort of religious 'superstitions.' One of the long-dreamed-for consequences of this would be the end of religiously motivated violence and division in society."[8]

A look at cults is proof enough that it has not happened. Additionally, according to Hunter, the struggle framing the public discourse about everything:

> abortion, child care, funding for the arts, affirmative action and quotas, gay rights, values in public education, or multiculturalism—[all] can be traced ultimately and finally to the matter of moral authority . . . [to wit,] the basis by which people determine whether something is good or bad, right or wrong, acceptable or unacceptable.[9]

Although most Americans occupy a middle ground, the debate has been polarized by organizations of various stripes struggling to set the national agenda on any of a series of special-interest or hot-button issues. The "personal disagreements that fire the culture wars," Hunter rightly observed,

> are deep and perhaps irreconcilable. *But these differences are often intensified and aggravated by the way they are presented to the public.* In brief, the media technology that makes public speech possible gives public discourse a life and logic of its own, a life and logic separated from the intentions of the speaker or the subtleties of arguments they employ.[10]

The irony of what Hunter described was that the forces that were setting in motion a shift away from the liberal arts as essentially culturally biased and politically incorrect, or as something that needed to be upheld at all costs to preserve the essence of Western society, were the very forces from which society needed protecting by the power of the liberal arts. Creating a framework for understanding, processing, and dealing with reality has been part of the human search for meaning for time immemorial. The dynamic tension between faith-based and rationalist traditions has formed the cornerstone for organizing the study of the liberal arts and human civilization in countless colleges and universities for years for this very reason.

The more society has changed, the more humans have had to process, the more they have had to adjust their understanding of reality and therefore their responses to it. Indeed, one need only consider the rapidity of change before the eighteenth century and since to appreciate that fact. And the closer we come to the present day, the quicker and more rapid the amount of change has become.

Sociologist Alvin Toffler addressed this issue in his book *Future Shock* some twenty-one years before Hunter identified the culture wars phenomenon. He wrote:

> The acceleration of change in our time is, itself, an elemental force. This accelerative thrust has personal and psychological, as well as sociological, consequences. . . . [U]nless man quickly learns to control the rate of change

in his personal affairs as well as in society at large, we are doomed to massive adaptational breakdown.[11]

Part of the issue was clearly tied to new technologies and the very rapidity of change they fostered. However, there was a corollary to the challenges being faced by modern people that, although related to technology, was independent of it. In earlier times, the public discourse was less immediate and thus more muted because of limitations imposed by time and geography.

There would have been no regular TV news reports or commercials designed to encourage sympathy for one or another political perspective. There would be no titillating blurring of celebrity and hard news. There would be no opportunity to speculate on the cause of a disaster or have a front-row seat to an unfolding tragedy half a continent or half a world away. The glaring disconnects between ideals and reality—be they in terms of issues of domestic or of international policies—would have been easier to ignore.

All those things were occurring pretty much simultaneously all over the world, as they always had, but now technology allows average citizens and decision makers alike to be fully aware of them. As a result, the gap between reality and self-perception—and the accepted narrative that gave it meaning—has grown exponentially, creating qualms and cognitive dissonance[12] that needed to somehow be resolved. The problem, Toffler observed, was that:

> Rational behavior . . . depends upon a ceaseless flow of data from the environment. It depends upon the power of the individual to predict, with at least fair success, the outcome of his own actions. To do that, he must be able to predict how the environment will respond to his acts. Sanity, itself, thus hinges on man's ability to predict his immediate, personal future on the basis of information fed him by the environment.
>
> When the individual is plunged into a fast and irregularly changing situation . . . predictive accuracy plummets. He can no longer make the reasonably correct assessments on which rational behavior is dependent.
>
> To compensate for this, to bring his accuracy up to the normal level again, he must scoop up and process far more information than before. And he must do it at extremely high rates of speed. In short, the more rapidly changing . . . the environment, the more information the individual needs to process in order to make effective, rational decisions.
>
> Yet, just as there are limits on how much sensory input we can accept, there are in-built constraints on our ability to process information.[13]

If this was true in 1970, it was even more so by the mid-1990s, to say nothing of the years since. As a result, people more and more readily have come to accept shorthand, preprocessed answers, and if those carry with them the ring of moral authority, to return to the thrust of Hunter's point, so much the better. By the 1990s, the moral choices had been roughly organized around two opposite approaches to determining right and wrong.

There were those who, in Hunter's words, were committed to "an external, definable, and transcendent authority."[14] In other words, they held fast to the immutable word of God contained in scripture, strictly interpreted. Such individuals had a hard time understanding people who they would characterize as liberal or worse. The other group Hunter described tended to "view truth as a process, as a reality that is ever unfolding," and moral authority as "resid[ing] in personal experience or scientific rationality."[15] Unfortunately, such folks had just as much difficulty understanding their more pious fellow citizens as the religiously minded did them.

The more morality has colored the discourse, the less civil the public discussion has become, because it is all too easy to compound James Madison's observation about the deleterious effects of fallible reason, self-love, and passions, with self-righteousness. This is especially true when new media outlets allow for heretofore unheard of audiences, ratings, or both.[16] It also permits posturing to become a substitute for substance, leaving many disenfranchised groups still powerless, frustrated, and marginalized.

Moreover, they are often not heard in any meaningful way, either by those ostensibly sympathetic to them—liberals who do not have to live in ghettoes, for example—or by those who themselves feel threatened by outgroups, like lower-middle- or working-class white males who face their own economic challenges and insecurities. Thus culture begets subculture as people seek ways of engineering manageable realities to meet their basic need "to predict how the environment will respond to . . . [their] acts," even if those predictions assume negative things about their fellow citizens, the world, or their place in it.

If culture matters in shaping the domestic discussion, the end of the Cold War made clear that it is also a central factor in international relations. As Samuel Huntington observed:

> In the post–Cold War world, culture is both a divisive and a unifying force. . . .
> The philosophical assumptions, underlying values, social relations, customs, and overall outlooks on life differ significantly among civilizations. The revitalization of religion throughout the world is reinforcing these cultural differences. Cultures can change, and the nature of their impact on politics and economics can vary from one period to another. Yet the major differences in political and economic development among civilizations are clearly rooted in their cultures.[17]

Ignoring that fact is dangerous. Globalization, which is driven by economic forces as well as innovations in technology, especially in the area of communications, has made international marketing of Western products—including culture in the form of music, movies, and clothes—ubiquitous. However, that does not translate into global homogenization around the Western idea, or even a Western way of life. If anything, these outward signs of Westernization mask a far more complex world order.

According to Huntington, "for the first time in history, global politics has become multipolar *and* multicivilizational."[18] Like groups within the United States, as Huntington astutely observed, "People [around the world] . . . are attempting to answer the most basic question that humans can face: Who are we? And they are answering that question in the traditional way that human beings have answered it, by reference to things that mean the most to them."[19]

The key word here is *basic*—it is built into the human psyche to seek meaning, purpose, order. If anything is universal, it is not the appeal of the so-called Western idea, but the need for a meaningful and understandable reality. Herein lies the heart of what a liberal arts education has sought to do for more than 2,500 years: to seek answers to the eternal questions, to challenge generations to think, to produce gadflies in the tradition of Socrates, who knew that the unexamined life was not worth living.

This is not a Western enterprise. It is a human one. The beginning of the end of history is not at hand, but rather the expansion of the very forces that have driven history since its outset. These include the human quest for meaning at its most fundamental level, something that has been going on everywhere around the world since time began. The only difference is that today, we have the ability to be privy to and learn from them, if we allow ourselves not to become distracted, but to be open and to ask the right questions—in essence, to internalize the values of liberal education.

This cannot be done using Google, nor is it neatly summarized in a Wikipedia article or with a tweet. Certainly, it was not something that could be satisfied either by capitulation to globalization (McWorld, in Barber's characterization), or by violent reaction to globalization (jihadism, in Barber's characterization).

There is even something vaguely ironic and not a little bit sinister in the fact that the forces of McWorld, as Barber suggested early on in the process, have been co-opted by those who were seeking to overthrow it.[20] At the risk of being overly dramatic, one might suggest that there were hints of Aldous Huxley's *A Brave New World* lurking in the shadows of McWorld that have since insinuated themselves more and more blatantly into mainstream culture, and in the process, now stand poised to destroy it.[21]

In November 2017, Chamath Palihapitiya, former vice-president of user growth at Facebook, said he felt "tremendous guilt" about helping to develop "tools that are ripping apart the social fabric of how society works." He told an audience at Stanford's Business School, "The short-term, dopamine-driven feedback loops that we have created are destroying how society works. No civil discourse, no cooperation, misinformation, mistruth." He went on to say that, "This is a global problem. It is eroding the core foundations of how people behave by and between each other."

Palihapitiya's statements came a day after Facebook president Sean Parker criticized the way his firm "exploit[s] a vulnerability in human psychology," and amid growing criticism of the media giant's role in tampering with the United States' 2016 presidential election. Parker was vocal about the effects that Facebook was having on the minds of children. The result was much hand wringing about the monster that he and his colleagues had unleashed upon the world.

Palihapitiya, meanwhile, told his audience to do some "soul-search[ing]" about their own relationship to social media. "Your behaviors, you don't realize it, but you are being programmed. It was unintentional, but now you gotta decide how much you're going to give up, how much of your intellectual independence [you are going to sacrifice]."[22]

Interestingly, there was nothing new here. Marie Winn wrote in 1977 about TV:

> The very nature of the television experience apart from the contents of the programs is rarely considered. Perhaps the ever-changing array of sights and sounds coming out of the machine—the wild variety of images meeting the eye and the barrage of human and inhuman sounds reaching the ear—fosters the illusion of a varied experience for the viewer. It is easy to overlook a deceptively simple fact: one is always *watching television* when one is watching television rather than having any other experience.[23]

In essence, the effect created a plug-in drug, which has since been augmented by other electronically powered drugs, like computers and cell phones.[24] But we would do well to avoid playing the victimization card, which is what happens when one fails to step back and ask hard questions, which is only possible if we take Palihapitiya's advice seriously and claim our "intellectual independence." Which brings us full circle to the power of the liberal arts, which force us to look at the big picture, to ask the hard questions, to consider issues in their broader historical, cultural, and humanistic context.

As Will Oremus observed in *Slate* on the heels of the Facebook revelations:

> We should all be more aware that companies are using our own psychological vulnerabilities against us because it helps us to be on our guard against overuse. But it's unrealistic, in our current capitalist environment, to expect Internet companies *not* to be working hard to insinuate their products into our lives in one way or another. That, for better or worse, is simply the prevailing business

model for online media. And with free services that sell us to advertisers as their real product, it is part of the bargain we have so far accepted.

So where does that leave us? Back where we started, essentially: Whether Facebook or any other app is good or bad for us doesn't just depend on *how much* we use it, but on *how* we use it—and what that usage does to us, both individually and as a society. Being addictive, in other words, doesn't make a company's products evil: Being evil makes them evil.[25]

It comes down to personal choice and responsibility—as it always has. The answer now, as 2,500 years ago, remains unchanged: a commitment to embracing the questions raised by the liberal arts, and understanding them in their fullest context, which open us to our true selves, our universe, and each other, and empowers us beyond our wildest dreams.

What H. G. Wells noted in the aftermath of World War I is even truer today:

> The need for a common knowledge of the general facts of human history throughout the world has become very evident during the tragic happenings of the last few years. Swifter means of communication have brought all men closer to one another for good or for evil. . . . A sense of history as the common adventure of all mankind is as necessary for peace within as it is for peace between the nations.[26]

If one needs *proof* that the liberal arts work, proof that knowledge is interconnected and historically and culturally grounded and must be taught and understood that way, proof that all this is not just a bunch of platitudes, consider where we would be on our "common adventure" without the achievements of those great thinkers who constitute the *longue durée*. And also remember the challenges that still need to be addressed because many of their lessons remain unlearned. It really is that simple.

Notes

PREFACE

1. Franklin D. Roosevelt, "Address at Oglethorpe University in Atlanta, Georgia," May 22, 1932, *The American Presidency Project*, accessed January 23, 2019, https://www.presidency.ucsb.edu/node/288094.

2. Franklin D. Roosevelt, "Inaugural Address," March 4, 1933, *The American Presidency Project*, accessed January 23, 2019, https://www.presidency.ucsb.edu/node/208712.

INTRODUCTION

1. Comments from "Student Focus Group on General Education," University of Lynchburg, 14 November 2013.

2. Ibid.

3. Troy H. to author, email, October 27, 2012.

4. Krista W., interview by author, Lynchburg, VA, October 16, 2014.

5. Nicole W., interview by author, Lynchburg, VA, December 4, 2014.

CHAPTER ONE

1. Robert H. Essenhigh, "A Few Thoughts on the Difference between Education and Training," *National Forum: The Phi Kappa Phi Journal* (Spring 2000): 46.

2. For an excellent discussion of this traditional distinction between the purposes of education and training, see Tracy Lee Simmons, *Climbing Parnassus: A New Apologia for Greek and Latin* (Wilmington, DE: ISI Books, 2002), 151–54.

3. Susan Wise Bauer, "What Is Classical Education?" *Classical Education for the Next Generation*, accessed October 31, 2014, http://www.welltrainedmind.com /classical-education/.

4. Nathan Hardin, "The End of the University as We Know It," *The American Interest* (January/February 2013), accessed February 12, 2013, http://www.the-american -interest.com/article.cfm?piece=1352.

5. Andy Chan and Tommy Derry, eds., "A Roadmap for Transforming the College-to-Career Experience," in *Rethinking Success: From the Liberal Arts to Careers in the 21st Century* (Winston-Salem, NC: Wake Forest University, 2013), 7.

6. Ibid.

7. Ibid., 9.

8. Richard Arum and Josipa Roksa, *Academically Adrift: Limited Learning on College Campuses* (Chicago: University of Chicago Press, 2011), 30.

9. Derek Bok, *Our Underachieving Colleges: A Candid Look at How Much Students Learn and Why They Should be Learning More* (Princeton, NJ: Princeton University Press, 2006), 8.

10. Arum and Roksa, *Academically Adrift*, 1–2.

11. Kenneth Bernstein, "Warnings from the Trenches" *Academe* 99, no. 1 (Jan.–Feb. 2013), accessed September 11, 2014, http://www.aaup.org/issue/january -february-2013.

12. Arum and Roksa, *Academically Adrift*, 91–92.

13. Ibid., 92.

14. Philip S. Babcock and Mindy Marks, "The Falling Time Cost of College: Evidence from Half a Century of Time Use Data," Working Paper 15954, National Bureau of Economic Research, Cambridge, MA, April 2010, 1.

15. Rebekah Nathan, *My Freshman Year: What a Professor Learned by Becoming a Student* (New York: Penguin Books, 2006), 113.

16. George Kuh, "What We Are Learning about Student Engagement," *Change* 35, no. 2 (March/April 2003): 28.

17. Arum and Roksa, *Academically Adrift*, 94–95.

18. Alexander Astin, *What Matters in College? Four Critical Years Revisited* (San Francisco: Jossey-Bass, 1993), 217.

19. James Engell and Anthony Dangerfield, *Saving Higher Education in the Age of Money* (Charlottesville, VA: University of Virginia Press, 2005), 5–6, and chapter 4.

20. *The Teaching of the Arts and Humanities at Harvard College: Mapping the Future* (May 2013), accessed September 16, 2014, http://artsandhumanities.fas.harvard .edu/files/humanities/files/mapping_the_future_31_may_2013.pdf; Commission on the Humanities and Social Sciences, *The Heart of the Matter: The Humanities and Social Sciences for a Vibrant, Competitive, and Secure Nation* (Cambridge, MA: American Academy of Arts and Sciences, 2013).

21. W. E. B. Dubois, *The Soul of Black Folk: Essays and Sketches* (Chicago: A. C. McClurg, 1907), 82.

22. Andrew Delbanco, *College: What It Was, Is, and Should Be* (Princeton, NJ: Princeton University Press, 2012), 99.

CHAPTER TWO

1. College Board, *Trends in College Pricing, 2014* (New York: College Board, 2014), 23.

2. Ibid., 24.

3. Tracey King and Ellynne Bannon, *The Burden of Borrowing: A Report on Rising Rates of Student Loan Debt* (Washington, DC: The State PIRG's Higher Education Project, 2002), 2.

4. Calculated using the Currency Calculator at MeasuringWorth.com, accessed January 28, 2019, https://www.measuringworth.com/calculators/uscompare/relative value.php.

5. Ibid.

6. The Institute for College Access and Success (TICAS), *Student Debt and the Class of 2013* (Oakland, CA: The Institute for College Access and Success, 2014), 1–2.

7. Ibid., 2.

8. William Shakespeare, *Hamlet* (New York: Simon and Schuster, 2012), 43.

9. TICAS, *Student Debt*, 1.

10. For more on college classifications, see: The Carnegie Classification of Institutions of Higher Learning, accessed May 10, 2015, http://carnegieclassifications. iu.edu/descriptions/; "Humanities Indicators: A Project of the American Academy of Arts and Sciences," accessed May 10, 2015, http://www.humanitiesindicators.org /content/document.aspx?i=396.

11. Kim Clark, "Colleges Play the Name Game," *US News and World Report*, September 17, 2009, accessed May 10, 2015, http://www.usnews.com/education /articles/2009/09/17/colleges-play-the-name-game.

12. Roger Dooley, "College Branding: The Tipping Point," *Forbes*, February 5, 2013, accessed May 9, 2015, http://www.forbes.com/sites/rogerdooley/2013/02/05 /college-branding-tipping/.

13. Rose Eveleth, "Academics Write Papers Arguing over How Many People Read (and Cite) Their Papers," *Smithsonian*, March 25, 2014, accessed May 10, 2015, http://www.smithsonianmag.com/smart-news/half-academic-studies-are-never-read -more-three-people-180950222/.

14. Dahlia Remler, "Are 90% of Academic Papers Really Never Cited? Reviewing the Literature on Academic Citations," The London School of Economics and Political Science, accessed May 10, 2015, http://blogs.lse.ac.uk/impactofsocial sciences/2014/04/23/academic-papers-citation-rates-remler/.

15. "How to Fix the Humanities," Minding the Campus: Reforming Our Universities, September 29, 2013, accessed May 10, 2015, http://www.mindingthecampus .org/2013/09/.

16. "Does Your Major Matter?" *Forbes*, October 29, 2012, accessed September 18, 2014, http://www.forbes.com/sites/collegeprose/2012/10/29/does-your-major-matter/.

17. Ecclesiastes 1:9, *The Holy Bible,* King James Version (New York: American Bible Society: 1999).

CHAPTER THREE

1. Richard Arum and Josipa Roksa, *Academically Adrift: Limited Learning on College Campuses* (Chicago: University of Chicago Press, 2011), 130.

2. Center of Inquiry, Wabash College, "Wabash National Study, 2006–2012," accessed September 23, 2014, http://www.liberalarts.wabash.edu/study-overview/.

3. Center of Inquiry, Wabash College, "High-Impact Practices and Experiences from the Wabash National Study," accessed September 23, 2014, http://www.liberal arts.wabash.edu/storage/High-Impact_Practices_Summary_2013-01-11.pdf.

4. Ibid.

5. George D. Kuh, *High-Impact Practices: What They Are, Who Has Access to Them, and Why They Matter* (Washington, DC: Association of American Colleges and Universities, 2008).

6. Jayne E. Brownell and Lynn E. Swaner, *Five High-Impact Practices: Research on Learning Outcomes, Completion, and Quality* (Washington, DC: Association of American Colleges and Universities, 2009).

7. George D. Kuh, Ken O'Donnell, *Ensuring Quality and Taking High-Impact Practices to Scale* (Washington, DC: Association of American Colleges and Universities, 2013).

8. National Leadership Council for Liberal Education and American Promise, *College Learning for the New Global Century* (Washington, DC: Association of American Colleges and Universities, 2007), 33.

9. Ibid., 34.

10. Gordon F. Vars, "Integrated Curriculum in Historical Perspective," *Educational Leadership* 49, no. 1 (October 1991): 14–15.

11. Eric Jensen, *Teaching with the Brain in Mind* (Alexandria, VA: Association for Supervision and Curriculum Development, 1998), 35.

12. Jean Radin, "Creating Enriched Learning Environments: Lessons from Brain Research," (November 2008), accessed September 30, 2014, http://www.elemental ethics.com/files/Radin_2.pdf; Pat Wolfe and Ron Brandt, "What Do We Know from Brain Research?" *Educational Leadership* 56, no. 3 (November 1998): 8–13.

13. Sasha A. Barab and Anita Landa, "Designing Effective Interdisciplinary Anchors," *Educational Leadership* 54, no. 6 (March 1997): 52–58; Daniel L. Kain, "Cabbages and Kings: Research Directions in Integrated/Interdisciplinary Curriculum," *The Journal of Educational Thought* 27, no. 3 (December 1993): 312–31.

14. Kain, "Cabbages and Kings."

15. John M. Eger, "Eliminating the Silos in Education," *Huffington Post*, September 30, 2014, accessed September 30, 2014, http://www.huffingtonpost.com/john-m-eger /eliminating-the-silos-in-_1_b_2155016.html.

16. Commission on the Humanities and Social Sciences, *The Heart of the Matter*, 10.

17. Ibid., 9.

18. Ibid., 10.

19. Ibid., 11.

20. Ibid., 12.

21. *The Teaching of the Arts and Humanities at Harvard College: Mapping the Future* (May 2013), accessed September 16, 2014, http://artsandhumanities.fas.harvard.edu/files/hum anities/files/mapping_the_future_31_may_2013.pdf, 2–3.

22. Ibid., 51.

23. Arum and Roksa, *Academically Adrift*, 88.

24. Stuart Rojstaczer and Christopher Healy, "Where A is Ordinary: The Evolution of American College and University Grading, 1940–2009," *Teachers College Record* 114, no. 7 (2012): 1–23.

25. Ibid., 89.

26. Plato, *Six Great Dialogues: Apology, Crito, Phaedo, Phaedrus, Symposium, The Republic* trans. Benjamin Jowett (Mineola, NY: Dover, 2007), 363.

27. Alfred North Whitehead, *The Aims of Education and Other Essays* (New York: The Free Press, 1967), 1.

28. John Newman, *The Idea of the University* (New Haven, CT: Yale University Press, 1996), 106.

29. Plato, *Six Great Dialogues*, 6.

30. Ibid., 18.

31. Ibid., 13.

32. James Madison, "Federalist No. 10," in *The Federalist Papers*, ed. Michael A. Genovese (New York: Palgrave MacMillan, 2009), 49–54.

33. Thomas Jefferson, *Notes on the State of Virginia* (New York: Penguin, 1999), 155.

34. Matthew Arnold, *Culture and Anarchy* (Cambridge, UK: Cambridge University Press, 1960), 6.

CHAPTER FOUR

1. Fernand Braudel and Sarah Matthews, *On History* (Chicago: University of Chicago Press, 1982).

2. Mortimer J. Adler, "The 103 Great Ideas: A Syntopical Approach to the Great Books," accessed January 28, 2019, http://www.thegreatideas.org/gi103.html; also see Mortimer J. Adler, *The Great Ideas: A Lexicon of Western Thought* (New York: Macmillan, 1992).

3. Mortimer J. Adler, *Six Great Ideas* (Los Angeles, CA: The Institute of Philosophical Research, 1981).

4. "Hebrews 11:1," *The Holy Bible*, King James Version (New York: American Bible Society, 1999).

5. Plato, *Six Great Dialogues: Apology, Crito, Phaedo, Phaedrus, Symposium, The Republic*, trans. Benjamin Jowett (Mineola, NY: Dover, 2007), 112.

6. Guy Claxton, "Expanding the Capacity to Learn: A New End for Education?" Opening Keynote Address, British Educational Research Association, Annual Conference, Warwick University, September 6, 2006, accessed December 14, 2014, http://www.learningtolearn.sa.edu.au/tfel/files/links/BERA_Keynote_Update_Feb1_2.pdf; Guy Claxton, *What's the Point of School? Rediscovering the Heart of Education*

(Oxford, UK: Oneworld, 2008); Guy Claxton, Maryl Chambers, Graham Powell, and Bill Lucas, *The Learning Powered School: Pioneering 21st Century Education* (Bristol, UK: TLO Limited, 2011); "Building Learning Power," accessed December 14, 2014, http://www.buildinglearningpower.co.uk/what_it_is.html.

7. College Parents of America, "Helping Your College Student Increase His Chances of Success," accessed December 14, 2014, http://www.collegeparents .org/members/resources/articles/helping-your-college-student-increase-his-chances -success.

CHAPTER FIVE

1. "How to Fix the Humanities," September 29, 2013, accessed January 28, 2019, http://www.mindingthecampus.org/2013/09/.

2. Edward O. Wilson, *Consilience: The Unity of Knowledge*, reprint ed. (New York: Vintage, 1999), 8.

3. Ibid., 11.

4. Quoted in Diogenes Laërtius, *Lives of the Eminent Philosophers*, Vol. 1, trans. Robert Drew Hicks (Cambridge, MA: Harvard University Press, 1925), 35.

5. Carnegie Foundation for the Advancement of Teaching, "The Carnegie Classification of Institutions of Higher Education," accessed October 22, 2014, http:// classifications.carnegiefoundation.org/.

CHAPTER SEVEN

1. Helen Barrett, "Plan for Five Careers in a Lifetime: Work is Impermanent—Reinvention is Rational," *Financial Times*, September 5, 2017, accessed February 1, 2019, https://www.ft.com/content/0151d2fe-868a-11e7-8bb1-5ba57d47eff7; Carl Bialik, "Seven Careers in a Lifetime? Think Twice, Researchers Say," *Wall Street Journal*, September 4, 2010, accessed February 1, 2019, https://www.wsj.com/articles /SB10001424052748704206804575468162805877990; Steve Denning, "How Many Careers Do You Get in a Lifetime?" *Forbes*, July 18, 2016, accessed February 1, 2019, https://www.forbes.com/sites/stevedenning/2016/07/18/how-many-careers -do-you-get-in-a-lifetime/#1f5f39f17556; Heather Long, "The New Normal: 4 Job Changes by the Time You're 32," *CNN Business*, April 12, 2016, accessed February 1, 2019, https://money.cnn.com/2016/04/12/news/economy/millennials-change-jobs -frequently/index.html; Jeanne Meister, "The Future of Work: Job Hopping Is the 'New Normal' for Millennials," *Forbes*, August 14, 2012, accessed February 1, 2019, https://www.forbes.com/sites/jeannemeister/2012/08/14/the-future-of-work-job-hop ping-is-the-new-normal-for-millennials/#3d0ee69813b8;" Jeffery R. Young, "How Many Times Will People Change Jobs? The Myth of the Endlessly Job-Hopping Millennial," *EdSurge: Digital Learning in Higher Ed*, July 20, 2017, accessed February

1, 2019, https://www.edsurge.com/news/2017-07-20-how-many-times-will-people
-change-jobs-the-myth-of-the-endlessly-job-hopping-millennial.

2. Denning, "How Many Careers."

3. Quoted in Long, "The New Normal."

CHAPTER EIGHT

1. Colleen Flaherty, "U Wisconsin–Stevens Point to Eliminate 13 Majors," *Inside Higher Education*, March 6, 2018, accessed January 28, 2019, https://www .insidehighered.com/quicktakes/2018/03/06/u-wisconsin-stevens-point-eliminate -13-majors.

2. UW–Stevens Point Proposes Adding, Cutting Programs to Prepare for Future, News Releases and Events, University Communications and Marketing, University of Wisconsin–Stevens Point, accessed January 28, 2019, https://www.uwsp.edu/ucm /news/Pages/Repositioning18.aspx.

3. Plato, *Six Great Dialogues*, 3.

4. James Davison Hunter, *Culture Wars: The Struggle to Define America* (New York: Basic Books, 1991).

5. Samuel P. Huntington, *The Clash of Civilizations and the Remaking of World Order* (New York: Touchstone, 1996).

6. Benjamin R. Barber, *Jihad vs. McWorld: How Globalism and Tribalism Are Reshaping the World* (New York: Ballantine Books, 1996).

7. Francis Fukuyama, "The End of History?" *The National Interest* (Summer 1989): 3–18; Francis Fukuyama, *The End of History and the Last Man* (New York: Avon Books, 1992).

8. Hunter, *Culture Wars*, 41.

9. Ibid., 42.

10. Ibid., 34.

11. Alvin Toffler, *Future Shock* (New York: Random House, 1970), 2.

12. Put simply, people feel uncomfortable when there is a disconnect between their perceived sense of themselves and their values, and of their actual behavior. Because the brain is wired to rationalize, it seeks to resolve the discomfort by justification, employing a host of defensive strategies designed to let the person hold on to his or her sense of self, including using selective "truths." See Robert Burton, *On Being Certain: Believing You Are Right Even When You're Not* (New York: St. Martin's Press, 2008); Cordelia Fine, *A Mind of Its Own: How Your Brain Distorts and De- ceives* (New York: W. W. Norton and Company, 2006); Leon Festinger, *A Theory of Cognitive Dissonance* (Stanford, CA: Stanford University Press, 1957); Eddie Harmon-Jones, *Cognitive Dissonance: Reexamining a Pivotal Theory in Psychol- ogy*, 2nd ed. (Washington, DC: American Psychological Association, 1999); Scott Plous, *The Psychology of Judgment and Decision Making* (New York: McGraw-Hill, 1993), chapter 3; Carol Tavris and Eliot Aaronson, *Mistakes Were Made (But Not by*

Me): Why We Justify Foolish Beliefs, Bad Decisions, and Hurtful Acts (New York: Mariner, 2008).

13. Toffler, *Future Shock*, 350–51. For more on information on sensory overload, also see Ithiel de Sola Pool, "Tracking the Flow of Information," *Science* 221 (August 1983): 609–13; Martin J. Epler and Jeanne Mengis, "The Concept of Information Overload: A Review of Literature from Organization Science, Accounting, Marketing, MIS, and Related Disciplines," *The Information Society: An International Journal,* 20 (May 2004): 325–44; Z. J. Lipowski, "Sensory and Information Inputs Overload: Behavioral Effects," *Comprehensive Psychiatry,* 16 (May–June 1975): 199–221; Charles A. O'Reilly III, "Individuals and Information Overload in Organizations: Is More Necessarily Better?" *Academy of Management Journal* 23 (December 1980): 684–96.

14. Hunter, *Culture Wars*, 44.

15. Ibid., 44–45.

16. Madison, "Federalist No. 10," 49.

17. Huntington, *The Clash of Civilizations*, 28–29.

18. Ibid., 21.

19. Ibid.

20. Barber, *Jihad vs. McWorld*, chapter 10.

21. Aldous Huxley, *A Brave New World* (New York: Harper and Brothers, 1932).

22. "Former Facebook Executive: Social Media is Ripping Society Apart," *The Guardian*, December 12, 2017, accessed February 2, 2019, https://www.theguardian .com/technology/2017/dec/11/facebook-former-executive-ripping-society-apart; Jared Gilmour, "Facebook is 'Destroying How Society Works' Says a Former Executive," *The Sacramento Bee*, December 11, 2017, accessed February 2, 2019, https://www.sacbee.com/news/nation-world/national/article189213899.html; Tom Huddleston, Jr. "Sean Parker Wonders What Facebook Is 'Doing to Our Children's Brains,'" *Fortune*, November 9, 2017, accessed February 2, 2019, http://fortune .com/2017/11/09/sean-parker-facebook-childrens-brains/; Rob Price, "Billionaire Ex-Facebook President Sean Parker Unloads on Mark Zuckerberg and Admits He Helped Build a Monster," *Business Insider*, November 9, 2017, accessed February 2, 2019, https://www.businessinsider.com/ex-facebook-president-sean-parker-social-network -human-vulnerability-2017-11; Garet Sloane, "Sean Parker Says Facebook Was Designed to be Addictive," *Ad Age*, November 9, 2017, accessed February 2, 2019, https://adage.com/article/digital/sean-parker-worries-facebook-rotting-children-s -brains/311238/; "Social Media 'Ripping Apart' Society, Former Facebook Executive Says," *CBS News*, December 12, 2017, accessed February 2, 2019, https://www .cbsnews.com/news/chamath-palihapitiya-former-facebook-executive-social-media -ripping-apart-society/.

23. Marie Winn, *The Plug-In Drug: Television, Computers, and Family Life*, 25th anniversary ed., rev. ed. (New York: Penguin, 2002), 3.

24. For more on the points made by Winn, Parker, and Palihapitiya see Robert H. Lustig, *The Hacking of the American Mind: The Science Behind the Corporate Takeover of Our Bodies and Brains* (New York: Avery, 2017).

25. Will Oremus, "Addiction for Fun and Profit: Facebook and Other Silicon Valley Companies Strive to Keep Users Hooked: Does That Make Them Evil?" *Slate*, November 10, 2017, accessed February 2, 2019, https://slate.com/technology /2017/11/facebook-was-designed-to-be-addictive-does-that-make-it-evil.html.

26. H. G. Wells, *The Outline of History: Being a Plain History of Life and Mankind* (New York: Macmillan, 1920), Introduction.

Bibliography

THE ART AND SCIENCE OF TEACHING AND LEARNING

Ambrose, Susan A., Michael W. Bridges, Michele DiPietro, Marsha C. Lovett, Marie K. Norman. *How Learning Works: Seven Research-Based Principles for Smart Teaching*. San Francisco, CA: John Wiley and Sons, 2010.

Association of American Colleges and Universities, *VALUE Rubrics*. Washington, DC: Association of American Colleges and Universities, 2010.

Association of American Colleges and Universities, "VALUE Rubric Development Project." https://www.aacu.org/value/rubrics.

Barab, Sasha A., and Anita Landa. "Designing Effective Interdisciplinary Anchors." *Educational Leadership* 54, no. 6 (March 1997): 52–58.

Barzun, Jacques. *Begin Here: The Forgotten Conditions of Teaching and Learning.* Chicago, IL: University of Chicago Press, 1991.

Barzun, Jacques. *Teacher in America.* Indianapolis, IN: Liberty Fund, 1981.

Bransford, John D., Ann L. Brown, and Rodney R. Cocking. *How People Learn: Brain, Mind, Experience and School.* Washington, DC: National Academy Press, 2000.

Brownell, Jayne E., and Lynn E. Swaner. *Five High-Impact Practices: Research on Learning Outcomes, Completion, and Quality.* Washington, DC: Association of American Colleges and Universities, 2009.

"Building Learning Power." http://www.buildinglearningpower.co.uk/what_it _is.html.

Butler, Nicholas Murray. *The Meaning of Education: Contributions to a Philosophy of Education.* Charleston, SC: Forgotten Books, 2012.

Center of Inquiry, Wabash College. "Wabash National Study, 2006–2012." http:// www.liberalarts.wabash.edu/study-overview/.

Center of Inquiry, Wabash College. "High-Impact Practices and Experiences from the Wabash National Study." http://www.liberalarts.wabash.edu/storage/High -Impact_Practices_Summary_2013-01-11.pdf.

Chandramohan, Balasubramanyam, and Stephen Fallows, eds. *Interdisciplinary Learning and Teaching in Higher Education.* New York: Routledge, 2008.

Claxton, Guy. "Expanding the Capacity to Learn: A New End for Education?" Opening Keynote Address, British Educational Research Association, Annual Conference, Warwick University, September 6, 2006. http://www.learningtolearn.sa.edu.au/tfel/files/links/BERA_Keynote_Update_Feb1_2.pdf.

Claxton, Guy. *What's the Point of School? Rediscovering the Heart of Education.* Oxford, UK: Oneworld, 2008.

Claxton, Guy, Maryl Chambers, Graham Powell, and Bill Lucas. *The Learning Powered School: Pioneering 21st Century Education.* Bristol, UK: TLO Limited, 2011.

College Parents of America. "Helping Your College Student Increase His Chances of Success." http://www.collegeparents.org/members/resources/articles/helping-your-college-student-increase-his-chances-success.

Driscoll, Marcy P. *Psychology of Learning for Instruction*, 3rd ed. Boston: Allyn and Bacon, 2003.

Eger, John M. "Eliminating the Silos in Education." *Huffington Post*, September 30, 2014. http://www.huffingtonpost.com/john-m-eger/eliminating-the-silos-in-_1_b_2155016.html.

Hartman, Hope J. "Scaffolding and Cooperative Learning." In *Human Learning and Instruction.* New York: City College of City University of New York, 2002.

Jensen, Eric. *Teaching with the Brain in Mind.* Alexandria, VA: Association for Supervision and Curriculum Development, 1998.

Kain, Daniel L. "Cabbages and Kings: Research Directions in Integrated/Interdisciplinary Curriculum." *The Journal of Educational Thought* 27, no. 3 (December 1993): 312–31.

Kuh, George D., Ken O'Donnell, et al. *Ensuring Quality and Taking High-Impact Practices to Scale.* Washington, DC: Association of American Colleges and Universities, 2013.

Kuh, George D. *High-Impact Practices: What They Are, Who Has Access to Them, and Why They Matter.* Washington, DC: Association of American Colleges and Universities, 2008.

Kuh, George D., Jillian Kinzie, Jennifer A. Buckely, Brian K. Bridges, and John C. Hayek. *What Matters to Student Success: A Review of the Literature.* Washington, DC: National Postsecondary Education Cooperative, 2006.

Kuh, George D., Jillian Kinzie, John H. Schuh, Elizabeth J. Whitt, et al. *Student Success in College: Creating Conditions That Matter.* San Francisco, CA: Jossey-Bass, 2005.

Lattuca, Lisa R., Lois J. Voigt, and Kimberly Q. Faith. "Does Interdisciplinarity Promote Learning? Theoretical Support and Research Questions." *The Review of Higher Education* 28, no. 1 (Fall 2004): 23–48.

McNair, Tia Brown, and Susan Albertine. "Seeking High-Quality, High-Impact Learning: The Imperative of Faculty Development and Curricular Intentionality." *Peer Review* 14, no. 3 (Summer 2012): 4–5.

National Survey of Student Engagement. *Experiences That Matter: Enhancing Student Learning and Success.* Bloomington: Center for Postsecondary Research, Indiana University Bloomington, 2007.

Paulson, Karen. "Faculty Perspectives of General Education and the Use of High-Impact Practices," *Peer Review* 14, no. 3 (Summer 2012): 25–28.

Radin, Jean. "Creating Enriched Learning Environments: Lessons from Brain Research." November 2008. http://www.elementalethics.com/files/Radin_2.pdf.

Tobias, Cynthia Ulrich. *The Way They Learn.* Wheaton, IL: Tyndale House, 1994.

Vars, Gordon F. "Integrated Curriculum in Historical Perspective," *Educational Leadership* 49, no. 2 (October 1991): 14–15.

Whitehead, Alfred North. *The Aims of Education and Other Essays.* New York: Free Press, 1967.

Wolfe, Pat, and Ron Brandt. "What Do We Know From Brain Research?" *Educational Leadership* 56, no. 3 (November 1998): 8–13.

Wood, Charlotte. "Researching and Developing Interdisciplinary Teaching: Towards a Conceptual Framework for Classroom Communication." *Higher Education* 54, no. 6 (2007): 853–66.

THE CURRENT STATE OF EDUCATION

American Council of Learned Societies. *Liberal Arts Colleges in American Higher Education: Challenges and Opportunities.* ACLS Occasional Paper No. 59. American Council of Learned Societies, New York, 2005.

Armstrong, Elizabeth A., and Laura T. Hamilton. *Paying for the Party: How College Maintains Inequality.* Reissue ed. Cambridge, MA: Harvard University Press, 2015.

Arum, Richard, and Josipa Roksa. *Academically Adrift: Limited Learning on College Campuses.* Chicago: University of Chicago Press, 2011.

Astin, Alexander. *What Matters in College? Four Critical Years Revisited.* San Francisco, CA: Jossey-Bass, 1993.

Astin, Alexander. "The Changing American College Student: Thirty Year Trends, 1966–1996," *Review of Higher Education* 21, no. 3 (Spring 1998): 115–35.

Augustine, Norman R. "One Cannot Live by Equations Alone: Education for Life in the Twenty-First Century." *Liberal Education* 99, no. 2 (Spring 2013): 14–21.

Bachelor's Degree Completions in the Humanities as a Percentage of All Bachelor's Degree Completions, 1948–2011, Humanities Indicators: A Project of the American Academy of Arts and Sciences. http://www.humanitiesindicators.org/content/indicatordoc.aspx?i=34.

Babcock, Philip S., and Mindy Marks. "The Falling Time Cost of College: Evidence from Half a Century of Time Use Data." Working Paper 15954, National Bureau of Economic Research, Cambridge, MA, April 2010.

Bastedo, Michael N., Philip G. Altbach, and Patricia J. Gumport, eds. *American Higher Education in the Twenty-First Century: Social, Political, and Economic Challenges,* 4th ed. Baltimore: Johns Hopkins University Press, 2016.

Bernstein, Kenneth. "Warnings from the Trenches," *Academe* 99, no. 1 (Jan.–Feb. 2013). http://www.aaup.org/issue/january-february-2013/.

Blumenstyk, Goldie. *American Higher Education in Crisis? What Everyone Needs to Know.* New York: Oxford University Press, 2015.

Bok, Derek. *Higher Education.* Cambridge, MA: Harvard University Press, 1986.

Bok, Derek. *Our Underachieving Colleges: A Candid Look at How Much Students Learn and Why They Should Be Learning More.* Princeton, NJ: Princeton University Press, 2006.

Boyer, Ernest L. *College: The Undergraduate Experience in America.* New York: Harper and Row, 1987.

Boyer, Ernest L. *Scholarship Reconsidered: Priorities of the Professoriate.* Stanford, CA: The Carnegie Foundation for the Advancement of Teaching, 1990.

Chan, Andy, and Tommy Derry, eds. *A Roadmap for Transforming the College-to-Career Experience.* Winston-Salem, NC: Wake Forest, 2013.

Clark, Kim. "Colleges Play the Name Game," *US News and World Report*, September 17, 2009. http://www.usnews.com/education/articles/2009/09/17/colleges-play-the-name-game.

College Board. *Trends in College Pricing, 2014.* New York: College Board, 2014.

"College Results Online." http://www.collegeresults.org/search1ba.aspx?institutionid=221014,233426,167996,152673,206589,203128,232609.

Cottom, Tressie McMillan. *Lower Ed: The Troubling Rise of For-Profit Colleges in the New Economy.* New York: The New Press, 2017.

David, Peter. "Inside the Knowledge Factory." *The Economist*, October 2, 1997. http://www.economist.com/node/600142.

Davidson, Cathy N. *The New Education: How to Revolutionize the University to Prepare Students for a World In Flux.* New York: Basic, 2017.

Dawson, Christopher. *The Crisis in Western Education.* Steubenville, OH: Franciscan University Press, 1989.

Delbanco, Andrew. *College: What It Was, Is, and Should Be.* Princeton, NJ: Princeton University Press, 2012.

Docking, Jeffrey R., and Carman C. Curton. *Crisis in Higher Education: A Plan to Save Small Liberal Arts Colleges in America.* East Lansing: Michigan State University, 2015.

"Does Your Major Matter?" *Forbes*, October 29, 2012. http://www.forbes.com/sites/collegeprose/2012/10/29/does-your-major-matter/.

Roger Dooley. "College Branding: The Tipping Point." *Forbes*, February 5, 2013. http://www.forbes.com/sites/rogerdooley/2013/02/05/college-branding-tipping/.

Engell, James, and Anthony Dangerfield. *Saving Higher Education in the Age of Money.* Charlottesville: University of Virginia Press, 2005.

Eveleth, Rose. "Academics Write Papers Arguing over How Many People Read (and Cite) Their Papers." *Smithsonian*, March 25, 2014. http://www.smithsonianmag.com/smart-news/half-academic-studies-are-never-read-more-three-people-180950222/.

Flaherty, Colleen. "U Wisconsin–Stevens Point to Eliminate 13 Majors." *Inside Higher Education*, March 6, 2018. https://www.insidehighered.com/quicktakes /2018/03/06/u-wisconsin-stevens-point-eliminate-13-majors.

Giamatti, A. Bartlett. *A Free and Ordered Space: The Real World of the University.* New York: W. W. Norton and Company, 1988.

Grigsby, Mary. *College Life through the Eyes of Students.* Albany: State University of New York Press, 2009.

Hanson, Victor Davis. "The Liberal Arts Weren't Murdered—They Committed Suicide." *The National Review*, December 18, 2018. https://www.nationalreview .com/2018/12/liberal-arts-education-politicized-humanities/.

Hardin, Nathan. "The End of the University as We Know It." *The American Interest* (January/February 2013). http://www.the-american-interest.com/article.cfm ?piece=1352.

Hart Research Associates. "It Takes More Than a Major: Employer Priorities for College Learning and Success." *Liberal Education* 99, no. 2 (Spring 2013): 22–29.

Higher Education Research Institute. *The American College Teacher: National Norms for 2007–2008.* Los Angeles: Higher Education Research Institute, University of California Los Angeles, 2009.

"How to Fix the Humanities," Minding the Campus: Reforming Our Universities, September 29, 2013. http://www.mindingthecampus.org/2013/09/.

Institute for College Access and Success. *Student Debt and the Class of 2013.* Oakland, CA: The Institute for College Access and Success, 2014.

Jennings, Nancy, Suzanne Lovett, Lee Cuba, Joe Swingle, and Heather Lindvist. "'What Would Make This a Successful Year for You?' How Students Define Success in College." *Liberal Education* 99, no. 2 (Spring 2013): 40–47.

Kerr, Clark. *The Use of the University.* Cambridge, MA: Harvard University Press, 2001.

King, Tracey, and Ellynne Bannon. *The Burden of Borrowing: A Report on Rising Rates of Student Loan Debt.* Washington, DC: The State PIRG's Higher Education Project, 2002.

Kronman, Anthony T. *Why Our Colleges and Universities Have Given Up on the Meaning of Life.* New Haven, CT: Yale University Press, 2007.

Kuh, George. "What We Are Learning about Student Engagement." *Change* 35, no. 2 (March/April 2003): 25–32.

Lagemann, Ellen Condliffe, and Harry Lewis, eds. *What Is College for? The Public Purpose of Higher Education.* New York: Teachers College Press, 2012.

Lingenfelter, Paul E. "American Education Second to None? How We Must Change to Meet Twenty-First Century Imperatives." *Liberal Education* 99, no. 2 (Spring 2013): 32–39.

MacTaggart, Terrence, ed. *Academic Turnarounds: Restoring Vitality to Challenged American Colleges and Universities.* Westport, CT: Praeger, 2007.

McGee, Jon. *Breakpoint: The Changing Marketplace for Higher Education.* Baltimore: Johns Hopkins University Press, 2015.

Menand, Louis. *The Marketplace of Ideas: Reform and Resistance in the American University.* New York: W. W. Norton, 2010.

Nathan, Rebekah. *My Freshman Year: What a Professor Learned by Becoming a Student.* New York: Penguin, 2006.

National Leadership Council for Liberal Education and America's Promise. *College Learning for the New Global Century.* Washington, DC: Association of American Colleges and Universities, 2007.

Pascarella, Ernest T., and Patrick T. Terenzini. *How College Affects Students: A Third Decade of Research.* San Francisco, CA: Jossey-Bass, 2005.

Pope, Loren. *Colleges That Change Lives: Forty Schools That Will Change the Way You Think About Colleges.* New York: Penguin, 2006.

Postman, Neil. *The End of Education: Redefining the Value of School.* New York: Vintage, 1996.

Remler Dahlia. "Are 90% of Academic Papers Really Never Cited? Reviewing the Literature on Academic Citations." The London School of Economics and Political Science. http://blogs.lse.ac.uk/impactofsocialsciences/2014/04/23/academic -papers-citation-rates-remler/.

Reuben, Julie A. *The Making of the Modern University: Intellectual Transformation and the Marginalization of Morality.* Chicago: University of Chicago Press, 1996.

Rojstaczer, Stuart, and Christopher Healy, "Where A Is Ordinary: The Evolution of American College and University Grading, 1940–2009." *Teachers College Record* 114, no. 7 (2012): 1–23.

Schneider, Carol Geary. "Losing Our Way on the Meanings of Student Success." *Liberal Education* 99, no. 2 (Spring 2013): 2–3.

Shares of All Bachelor's Degrees Awarded in Selected Academic Fields, 1987–2010, Humanities Indicators: A Project of the American Academy of Arts and Sciences. http://www.humanitiesindicators.org/content/indicatordoc.aspx?i=34.

US News and World Report, *US News College Rankings and Reports.* https://www .usnews.com/best-colleges.

"UW–Stevens Point Proposes Adding, Cutting Programs to Prepare for Future," News Releases and Events, University Communications and Marketing, University of Wisconsin–Stevens Point. https://www.uwsp.edu/ucm/news/Pages/Reposition ing18.aspx.

LIBERAL ARTS AND THE NATURE OF KNOWLEDGE

Adler, Mortimer J. *A Guidebook to Learning: For a Lifelong Pursuit of Wisdom.* New York: Macmillan, 1986.

Adler, Mortimer J. *How to Think about the Great Ideas: From the Great Books of Western Civilization.* Chicago: Open Court, 2000.

Adler, Mortimer J. *Six Great Ideas.* Los Angeles: Institute of Philosophical Research, 1981.

Adler, Mortimer J. *The Great Ideas: A Lexicon of Western Thought.* Norwalk, CT: Easton, 2001.

Adler, Mortimer J. "The 103 Great Ideas: A Syntopical Approach to the Great Books." http://www.thegreatideas.org/gi103.html.

Adler, Mortimer J., ed. *The Paideia Program: An Educational Syllabus.* Los Angeles: Institute of Philosophical Research, 1984.

American Academy of Arts and Sciences. *The Heart of the Matter: The Humanities and Social Sciences for a Vibrant, Competitive, and Secure Nation.* Cambridge, MA: American Academy of Arts and Sciences, 2013.

Anders, George. *You Can Do Anything: The Surprising Power of a "Useless" Liberal Arts Education.* New York: Little Brown, 2017.

Arnold, Matthew. *Culture and Anarchy.* Cambridge, UK: Cambridge University Press, 1960.

Babbitt, Irving. *Literature and the American College: Essays in Defense of the Humanities.* Washington, DC: National Humanities Institute, 1986.

Barzun, Jacques. *The Culture We Deserve: A Critique of Disenlightenment.* Middletown, CT: Wesleyan University Press, 1989.

Bauer, Susan Wise. "What Is Classical Education?" *Classical Education for the Next Generation.* http://www.welltrainedmind.com/classical-education/.

DeMille, Oliver. *A Thomas Jefferson Education: Teaching a Generation of Leaders for the Twenty-First Century.* Cedar City, UT: George Wythe College Press, 2006.

Dharmsi, Karim, and James Zimmer, eds. *Liberal Education and the Idea of the University: Arguments and Reflections on Theory and Practice.* Wilmington, DE: Vernon, 2019.

Dolby, Nadine. "The Decline of Empathy and the Future of Liberal Education." *Liberal Education* 99, no. 2 (Spring 2013): 60–64.

Durant, Will. *The Greatest Minds and Ideas of All Time.* New York: Simon and Schuster, 2002.

Durant, Will. *The Story of Philosophy: The Lives and Opinions of the World's Greatest Philosophers.* New York: Simon and Schuster, 1926.

Durant, Will, and Ariel Durant. *The Lessons of History.* New York: Simon and Schuster, 1968.

Caldecott, Stratford. *Beauty for Truth's Sake: On the Re-enchantment of Education.* Grand Rapids, MI: Brazo, 2009.

Essenhigh, Robert H. "A Few Thoughts on the Difference between Education and Training." *National Forum: The Phi Kappa Phi Journal* (Spring 2000): 46.

Fassbinder, Samuel Day, Anthony J. Nocella II, and Richard Kahn, eds. *Greening the Academy: Ecopedagogy through the Liberal Arts.* Rotterdam, NL: Sense, 2012.

Ferrall, Victor E. Jr. *Liberal Arts at the Brink.* Cambridge, MA: Harvard University Press, 2011.

Hanson, Victor Davis, John Heath, and Bruce S. Thornton. *Bonfire of the Humanities: Rescuing the Classics in an Impoverished Age.* Wilmington, DE: Intercollegiate Studies Institute, 2000.

Hicks, David V. *Norms and Nobility: A Treatise on Education.* Lanham, MD: University Press of America, 1999.

Hirsch, E. D., Jr. *Cultural Literacy: What Every American Needs to Know.* New York: Houghton Mifflin, 1987.

Marber, Peter, and Daniel Araya, eds. *The Evolution of Liberal Arts in the Global Age.* New York: Routledge, 2017.

Martin, Everett Dean. *The Meaning of a Liberal Education.* New York: W. W. Norton and Company, 1926.

Newman, John Henry. *The Idea of a University.* New Haven, CT: Yale University Press, 1996.

Nussbaum, Martha C. *Cultivating Humanity: A Classical Defense of Reform in Liberal Education.* Cambridge, MA: Harvard University Press, 1997.

Nussbaum, Martha C. *Not for Profit: Why Democracy Needs the Humanities.* Princeton, NJ: Princeton University Press, 2010.

Roth, Michael S. *Beyond the University: Why Liberal Education Matters.* New Haven, CT: Yale University Press, 2014.

Simmons, Tracy Lee. *Climbing Parnassus: A New Apologia for Greek and Latin.* Wilmington, DE: Intercollegiate Studies Institute, 2007.

Stross, Randall. *A Practical Education: Why Liberal Arts Majors Make Great Employees.* Stanford, CA: Stanford University Press, 2017.

The Teaching of the Arts and Humanities at Harvard College: Mapping the Future (May 2013). http://artsandhumanities.fas.harvard.edu/files/humanities/files/mapping_the_future_31_may_2013.pdf.

Van Doren, Mark. *Liberal Education.* Boston: Beacon, 1959.

Veith, Gene Edward Jr., and Andrew Kern. *Classical Education: The Movement Sweeping America.* Washington, DC: Capital Research Center, 2001.

Wilson, Edward O. *Consilience: The Unity of Knowledge.* New York: Vintage, 1999.

Wren, J. Thomas, Ronald E. Riggio, and Michael A. Genovese, eds. *Leadership and the Liberal Arts: Achieving the Promise of a Liberal Education.* New York: Palgrave Macmillan, 2009.

Zakaria, Fareed. *In Defense of a Liberal Education.* New York: W. W. Norton, 2015.

SOME HISTORICAL, SOCIOLOGICAL, AND PSYCHOLOGICAL PERSPECTIVES

Barber, Benjamin R. *Jihad vs. McWorld: How Globalism and Tribalism Are Reshaping the World.* New York: Ballantine, 1996.

Barrett, Helen. "Plan for Five Careers in a Lifetime: Work is Impermanent—Reinvention is Rational." *Financial Times,* September 5, 2017. https://www.ft.com/content/0151d2fe-868a-11e7-8bb1-5ba57d47eff7.

Bialik, Carl. "Seven Careers in a Lifetime? Think Twice, Researchers Say." *The Wall Street Journal,* September 4, 2010. https://www.wsj.com/articles/SB10001424052748704206804575468162805877990.

Braudel, Fernand, and Sarah Matthews. *On History.* Chicago: The University of Chicago Press, 1982.

Burton, Robert. *On Being Certain: Believing You Are Right Even When You're Not.* New York: St. Martin's Press, 2008.

Cohen, Arthur, and Carrie B. Kisker. *The Shaping of American Higher Education: Emergence and Growth of the Contemporary System,* 2nd ed. San Francisco: Jossey-Bass, 2010.

Denning, Steve. "How Many Careers Do You Get in A Lifetime?" *Forbes*, July 18, 2016. https://www.forbes.com/sites/stevedenning/2016/07/18/how-many-careers -do-you-get-in-a-lifetime/#1f5f39f17556.

de Sola Pool, Ithiel. "Tracking the Flow of Information." *Science* 221 (August 1983): 609–13.

Dubois, W. E. B. *The Soul of Black Folk: Essays and Sketches*. Chicago: A. C. Mc-Clurg, 1907.

Epler, Martin J., and Jeanne Mengis. "The Concept of Information Overload: A Review of Literature from Organization Science, Accounting, Marketing, MIS, and Related Disciplines." *The Information Society: An International Journal* 20 (May 2004): 325–44.

Festinger, Leon. *A Theory of Cognitive Dissonance*. Stanford: Stanford University Press, 1957.

Fine, Cordelia. *A Mind of Its Own: How Your Brain Distorts and Deceives*. New York: W. W. Norton and Company, 2006.

"Former Facebook Executive: Social Media Is Ripping Society Apart." *The Guardian*, December 12, 2017. https://www.theguardian.com/technology/2017/dec/11 /facebook-former-executive-ripping-society-apart.

Fukuyama, Francis. "The End of History?" *The National Interest* (Summer 1989): 3–18.

Fukuyama, Francis. *The End of History and the Last Man*. New York: Avon, 1992.

Gilmour, Jared. "Facebook Is 'Destroying How Society Works' Says a Former Executive." *The Sacramento Bee*, December 11, 2017. https://www.sacbee.com /news/nation-world/national/article189213899.html.

Harmon-Jones, Eddie. *Cognitive Dissonance: Reexamining a Pivotal Theory in Psychology*, 2nd ed. Washington, DC: American Psychological Association, 1999.

Huddleston, Tom, Jr. "Sean Parker Wonders What Facebook Is 'Doing to Our Children's Brains.'" *Fortune*, November 9, 2017. http://fortune.com/2017/11/09/sean -parker-facebook-childrens-brains/.

Hunter, James Davison. *Culture Wars: The Struggle to Define America*. New York: Basic,1991.

Huntington, Samuel P. *The Clash of Civilizations and the Remaking of World Order*. New York: Touchstone, 1996.

Jaspers, Karl. Origin and Goal of History. London, UK: Routledge and Kegan Paul, 1953.

Jefferson, Thomas. *Notes on the State of Virginia*. New York: Penguin, 1999.

Kliebard, Herbert M. *The Struggle for the American Curriculum, 1893–1958*, 3rd ed. New York: Routledge, 2004.

Laërtius, Diogenes. *Lives of the Eminent Philosophers*, Vol. 1. Trans. Robert Drew Hicks. Cambridge, MA: Harvard University Press, 1925.

Lipowski, Z. J. "Sensory and Information Inputs Overload: Behavioral Effects." *Comprehensive Psychiatry* 16 (May–June 1975): 199–221.

Long, Heather. "The New Normal: 4 Job Changes By the Time You're 32." *CNN Business*, April 12, 2016. https://money.cnn.com/2016/04/12/news/economy /millennials-change-jobs-frequently/index.html.

Lustig, Robert H. *The Hacking of the American Mind: The Science Behind the Corporate Takeover of Our Bodies and Brains.* New York: Avery, 2017.

Meister, Jeanne. "The Future of Work: Job Hopping Is the 'New Normal' for Millennials." *Forbes*, August 14, 2012. https://www.forbes.com/sites/jeannemeister /2012/08/14/the-future-of-work-job-hopping-is-the-new-normal-for-millennials /#3d0ee69813b8.

Merlyn, Vaughan. "Why Efforts to Break Down Silos Fail and What Business Relationship Managers Can Do about It." Business Relationship Management Institute, November 5, 2013. http://brminstitute.org/why-efforts-to-break-down-silos-fail -and-what-brm-can-do-about-it/.

O'Reilly, Charles A., III. "Individuals and Information Overload in Organizations: Is More Necessarily Better?" *Academy of Management Journal* 23 (December 1980): 684–96.

Oremus, Will. "Addiction for Fun and Profit: Facebook and Other Silicon Valley Companies Strive to Keep Users Hooked: Does That Make Them Evil?" *Slate*, November 10, 2017. https://slate.com/technology/2017/11/facebook-was-designed -to-be-addictive-does-that-make-it-evil.html.

Plato. *Six Great Dialogues: Apology, Crito, Phaedo, Phaedrus, Symposium, The Republic.* Trans. Benjamin Jowett. Mineola, NY: Dover, 2007.

Plous, Scott. *The Psychology of Judgment and Decision Making.* New York: McGraw-Hill, 1993.

Price, Rob. "Billionaire Ex-Facebook President Sean Parker Unloads on Mark Zuckerberg and Admits He Helped Build a Monster." *Business Insider*, November 9, 2017. https://www.businessinsider.com/ex-facebook-president-sean-parker-social -network-human-vulnerability-2017-11.

"Social Media 'Ripping Apart' Society, Former Facebook Executive Says." *CBS News*, December 12, 2017. https://www.cbsnews.com/news/chamath-palihapitiya -former-facebook-executive-social-media-ripping-apart-society/.

Tavris, Carol, and Eliot Aaronson. *Mistakes Were Made (But Not by Me): Why We Justify Foolish Beliefs, Bad Decisions, and Hurtful Acts.* New York: Mariner, 2008.

Thelin, John R. *A History of American Higher Education,* 2nd ed. Baltimore, MD: Johns Hopkins University Press, 2004.

Toffler, Alvin. *Future Shock.* New York: Random House, 1970.

Winn, Marie. *The Plug-In Drug: Television, Computers, and Family Life,* 25th anniversary ed. New York: Penguin, 2002.

Wells, H. G. *The Outline of History: Being a Plain History of Life and Mankind.* New York: Macmillan, 1920.

Young, Jeffery R. "How Many Times Will People Change Jobs? The Myth of the Endlessly Job-Hopping Millennial." *EdSurge: Digital Learning in Higher Ed,* July 20, 2017. https://www.edsurge.com/news/2017-07-20-how-many-times-will -people-change-jobs-the-myth-of-the-endlessly-job-hopping-millennial.

Lightning Source UK Ltd.
Milton Keynes UK
UKHW010020110920
369708UK00001B/1